THE EXPLORATIONS OF
ANTARCTICA

Jenny Island (oil)

OPPOSITE RRS *Bransfield* moored at Brunt Ice Shelf (oil)

THE EXPLORATIONS OF
ANTARCTICA

The Last Unspoilt Continent

Professor G. E. Fogg and David Smith

CASSELL

To The British Antarctic Survey

Cassell Publishers Limited
Villiers House, 41/47 Strand, London WC2N 5JE

Copyright 1990 © Text: Professor G. E. Fogg   Illustrations: David Smith

First published 1990

Distributed in the United States by
Sterling Publishing Co. Inc.
387 Park Avenue South, New York, NY 10016–8810

Distributed in Australia by
Capricorn Link (Australia) Pty Ltd
PO Box 665, Lane Cove, NSW 2066

British Library Cataloguing in Publication Data
Fogg, G. E. (Gordon Elliott)
    The explorations of Antarctica: the last unspoilt continent.
    1. Antarctic. Exploration, history
    I. Title   II. Smith, David
    919.8'904

ISBN 0–304–31813–2

Typeset by August Filmsetting, Haydock, St Helens
Printed and bound in Spain by Graficas Reunidas

Contents

Ice-floes, Weddell Sea (oil)

Foreword by
His Royal Highness
The Duke of Edinburgh
KG KT

BUCKINGHAM PALACE.

Books, articles, statistics, films and photographs can tell us a lot about the remote areas of the world, but there is nothing quite like a series of paintings by a sympathetic artist to give the feeling of a place. Constable, Turner and Seago, amongst others, had the capacity to convey the atmosphere of the landscape and to bring it alive.

Only Edward Wilson, an amateur who did many water-colours while he was in the Antarctic with Scott on his last expedition, and Edward Seago, a professional artist who came with me to the southern ocean in the Royal Yacht Britannia in 1957, had the opportunity to capture the very special nature of the Antarctic before David Smith was invited to record his impressions by the British Antarctic Survey.

In this book, a selection of his evocative pictures is set in the context of exploration and scientific research by Professor Fogg, who has also worked in the Antarctic as a guest of the Survey.

The greatest value of the Antarctic is the contribution it can make to human understanding of the evolution and workings of our planet. I hope that this book will help to create greater awareness of the true nature of this forbidding continent and to promote the will to protect this last major wilderness area from human disturbance and exploitation.

Introduction
by Lord Shackleton

THERE ARE MANY excellent books on the Antarctic but this one, by Professor Fogg and David Smith, is special. What is so impressive about *The Explorations of Antarctica* is that, firstly, it contains David Smith's paintings, which truly are wonderful, evocative and accurate. Indeed, I once described David as 'the finest recorder of that continent this century'. And secondly, not only do we have David's superb oil and water-colour portraits of the seventh continent, an incredibly beautiful part of the world, but his paintings are accompanied by Professor Fogg's highly sophisticated and intelligent text. Tony Fogg was Chairman of the Scientific Advisory Committee of the British Antarctic Survey for many years, and knows the area well. As does David, who has been there more than once to paint.

There is in Professor Fogg's text the most vivid description of the Antarctic to match David Smith's illustrations, combined with an almost unique historical dimension: a careful blending of the past right back to a time when the continent was a myth. From the early adventurers to the scientists and explorers of modern times – including, of course, those great journeys by Scott, Shackleton and Amundsen – the text presents a balanced and informed account of our least-known continent.

This book is dedicated to giving an accurate picture, both written and painted, of that lovely, vulnerable land – the Antarctic. I need not attempt to describe the place itself because it is so well described in the book, but it is as much a source of potential political trouble as it is an important source of scientific information. For example, the ozone 'hole' in the lower edge of the stratosphere was found by the British Antarctic Survey in 1981 without the help of satellites though, of course, it has been confirmed by satellite since.

The actual South Pole is an extraordinary spot. It was well described by

Captain Scott as 'this awful place'. I went there the easy way. I was flown by the Americans to their base. The base commander said: 'Take a look at that horizon and then the other way.' I did, and he asked: 'What do you see?'

I replied: 'Well, that horizon is just a little bit nearer.'

And he said, 'Yes, the ice is moving at one half a centimetre a day, nearly two metres (six feet) a year.'

The natural phenomena of the Antarctic are of immense scientific interest. We have learned a little; I hope we shall learn more about the atmospheric history of the earth and many other aspects. The important question for all of us is: can we conserve the Antarctic?

There are a number of potentially hazardous conflicting territorial claims to the Antarctic, including those of the British, the Argentinians, the Chileans, the Australians, the New Zealanders and the Norwegians. The overlapping claims have not yet been solved, but they have been frozen, in one of the most remarkable treaties in history. The British played a very large part in developing a treaty that, in effect, as is described fully in the book, ensures that the Antarctic is the one part of the world to which the cold war has never come. Furthermore, the overlapping claims of the Chileans, the Argentinians and the British are in cold storage, whatever action is taken.

The most important, and highly cost-effective, scientific work has undoubtedly been done in the seventh continent by the British Antarctic Survey. This work, in co-operation with other countries like Argentina, has led to the Minerals Convention. Those of us who desperately wish to preserve the Antarctic regard the Convention as the best guarantee of preventing uncontrolled exploitation. Indeed, it makes it very difficult to have any mineral exploration at all. To have a self-limiting agreement of this nature amongst all the nations is unprecedented.

The Antarctic Treaty and the Antarctic Convention on Minerals are therefore extremely important both for conserving the Antarctic habitat and for the peace of the continent. We ought not to think that the Antarctic, beautiful and unspoilt as it still is, is without political danger for the rest of the world. It is, in my opinion, important that the Convention be ratified, even though the Australians have so far refused to do so, because it is part of our building up a 'whole' view of the Antarctic which, valuably, belongs to the whole world and needs to be preserved for the whole world. The Australians pursue their admirable dream of turning the Antarctic into a world park – a case, I believe, of best being the enemy of good.

This book is intended to highlight the need for conservation. I believe it will contribute to the understanding of many people by outlining and explaining the enduring fascination of the Antarctic, while seeking to ensure that sound environmental policies are followed.

Sunset, Mount Tumbledown, Port Stanley (water-colour)

Acknowledgements

WE WISH firstly to express our gratitude to His Royal Highness The Duke of Edinburgh for his kindness in providing a Foreword for this book. We are also deeply grateful to Lord Shackleton for writing his most encouraging and sympathetic Introduction.

The dedication acknowledges our debt of gratitude to those who made the book possible in the first place. It was David Limbert, sometime meteorologist with the British Antarctic Survey, who had the idea that David Smith should visit Antarctica and thereby provided the inspiration for a book illustrated with his pictures. Dr R. M. Laws FRS, Director of the Survey until 1987, took up the suggestion enthusiastically and both he and his predecessor, Sir Vivian Fuchs FRS, were equally encouraging in involving Tony Fogg in the scientific work of the Survey. Thus introduced into the company of 'Fids', we were both accepted with the utmost friendliness and given all possible assistance in carrying out our respective activities on sea and shore. We are immensely grateful, not only for having been given the opportunity to experience the Antarctic at first hand, but for being admitted into a congenial fraternity in which it was taken as a matter of course that the arts and sciences are but two ways of looking at the same thing.

The writing of the book and its illustration with historic pictures would not have been possible without access to the library of the Scott Polar Research Institute and our thanks must be expressed to its Director for permission to reproduce material from the Institute's collections and to its library staff, in particular Harry King and Robert Headland, for their unstinted help at all times. We are similarly grateful to the Director of the Royal Botanic Gardens, Kew, for permission to use material in the Garden's archives and to its library staff for their assistance in locating it. Our gratitude must also be expressed to the following who have kindly given permission to use material from published works: John Murray (Publishers) Ltd (quotations from F. Debenham's *In the Antarctic*), Cambridge University Press (quotations from R. D. Keynes (ed.) *The Beagle Record*), Sir Vivian Fuchs (a quotation from his *Of Ice and Men*), News Limited of Australia (a quotation from *The Australian*), Mrs Angela Mathias (quotations from *The Worst Journey in the World*), Scott Polar Research Institute (quotations from Edward Wilson's *Diary of the Discovery Expedition* and *Diary of the Terra Nova Expedition*, published by Blandford Press), the *Geographical Magazine* (a quotation from an article by David Smith), Macmillan New York (quotations from R. C. Murphy's *Logbook for Grace*), G. P. Putnam's Sons (a quotation from R. E. Byrd's *Alone*), and Muller, Blond and White Ltd (quotations from J. E. Darlington's *My Antarctic Honeymoon*). Our thanks are also due to the Master of Dulwich College for his permission to reproduce the painting by Norman Wilkinson. While we have done our best to locate all the copyright owners of the material we have used it may be that we have missed some and to any such we tender our apologies. Our thanks also to all those who own the paintings by David Smith featured in this book.

Finally, we are extremely grateful to Helen Dwyer, who searched out and photocopied much recondite material; Brenda Thake and Timothy Fogg, who read and constructively criticized sections of the manuscript; William Rowntree, for his impeccable photography; Kerry Cuthbertson, who so expertly converted the rough draft into typescript; Amanda Little, who sustained our belief that it was worth publishing; my publisher Jonathan Grimwood, for his great help and understanding, and Miranda Walker for seeing the book through the press.

G. E. 'Tony' Fogg
David Smith

The world map of
Orontius Finaeus, 1531.
This was drawn shortly
after Magellan had sailed
through the strait which
bears his name, when
Tierra del Fuego was
thought to be part of a
large southern continent,
and is the first to use the
designation Terra Austra-
lis Incognita. It is remarkable how nearly the actual
shape of the continent has
been predicted. (Courtesy
of the Scott Polar Research
Institute)

Chapter One

Discovery

S ATELLITE PHOTOGRAPHS show our earth as a glimmering sphere of ultramarine, pearly white and soft greens and browns – a jewel among planets. At the bottom, there because of northern prejudice and not for any absolute reason, we see Antarctica, showing through an encircling band of cloud and separated from the everyday world by a wide expanse of ocean. It is a continent of nearly 14 million square kilometres, (5½ million square miles), larger than Europe but smaller than South America. Its effective area is much larger than this because it is surrounded by sea-ice which grows from some 3 million square kilometres (1 million square miles) in February, the end of summer, to about 20 million square kilometres (7½ million square miles) in September, the end of winter. All but about 1 per cent of the Antarctic land mass is itself covered with ice, which in places is about 5 kilometres (3 miles) thick and which contains 90 per cent of the world's fresh water. Not surprisingly, then, Antarctica is the coldest place on earth with temperatures that fall to −89°C (−128°F).

Although the northern Arctic, too, is cold and ice-bound, Antarctica is different in being a land-mass surrounded by sea, whereas the North Pole is set in an ocean surrounded by lands which have given plants, animals and man a means of closer approach than is possible in the south.[1] This isolation has led to Antarctica's politics being as unique as its physical geography. Because no one else has had much idea of what to do with it, Antarctica has so far been left to explorers and scientists, who, through a combination of luck and judgement, have evolved a system for its management which has enabled otherwise antipathetic nationalities to co-exist

15

and work together harmoniously in an area where sovereignty and law have little meaning. For most scientists who have worked there, Antarctica has a value beyond that of the scientific data which can be extracted from it. The satisfaction derived from sharing interests and facing a hostile environment with select companions and a minimum of bureaucratic interference form one element in this. Another is the impact of the austere and unspoilt loveliness of Antarctica itself. To get a rounded view of this remarkable part of our planet, collaboration is needed between artist and scientist, and that is what we have attempted in this book. Our different approaches, after all, have much in common; we both strive to give a simplified but valid representation of what we observe.

The thousands of miles of turbulent ocean and the wide, booby-trapped, sea-ice defences have effectively kept man away from Antarctica until the last two or three hundred years. Antarctica never has had native human inhabitants. It may be, however, that its defences were first probed not by European technology but by Polynesian daring. A Rarotongan legend recounts a voyage made by one Ui-te-Rangiora into a region of fogs, monstrous seas and what seem to have been icebergs and brash ice (small ice fragments).[2] Be this as it may – and it is rather odd that intense cold is not mentioned in the story – it was Francis Drake in 1578 who made the first historically recorded incursion into these seas.

As soon as Europeans realized that the earth is round they had to envisage what there might be in the far south. Some geographers, feeling that there must be a counterpoise for the large and populous continents, placed a 'Terra Australis Incognita', peopled with a teeming and wealthy population, in the southern hemisphere. The map of Orontius Finaeus, first published in 1531, showed a vast southern continent stretching well into temperate latitudes and closely approaching South America. Magellan, in the course of his circumnavigation, proved that there was no actual connection, but he did see land to the south as he sailed through the straits leading from the Atlantic to the Pacific Ocean which he had discovered. Following him, Drake, after clearing the Magellan Straits, was driven to the south of the islands of Tierra del Fuego by a storm and, as his chaplain Francis Fletcher recounted in his book *The World Encompassed* (1628), found that:

The uttermost cape or hedland of all these Ilands, stands neere in 56 deg. without which there is no maine, nor Iland to be seene to the Southwards: but that the Atlanticke Ocean, and the South sea, meete in a most large and free scope.

It hath beene a dreame through many ages, that these Ilands have been a maine, and that it hath beene *terra incognita*; wherein many strange monsters lived. Indeed it might truly, before this time, be called *incognita*, for howsover the mappes and generall descriptions of *Cosmographers*, either upon the deceiveable reports of other men, or the deceitful imaginations of themselves (supposing never herein to be corrected) have set it downe, yet it is true, that before this time, it was never discovered, or certainely knowne by any traveller, that wee have heard of.[3]

In spite of this, belief in a southern continent with a pleasant climate and teeming inhabitants persisted for almost another two hundred years. The voyage of the astronomer Edmond Halley into the South Atlantic in 1699–1700 was for a specifically scientific purpose, a survey of magnetic variation, but he was given permission by the Admiralty to seek for 'South unknown lands, between Magellan Streights and the Cape of Good Hope'. Getting among icebergs just north of South Georgia, he decided that the health and safety of his crew came first and gave up further search.[4] However, it so happened that the discoveries of the few other voyagers who ventured into the Southern Ocean in this period seemed to confirm the idea of a continent. The Dutch navigator Jacob Roggeveen, sailing in the Pacific, reached a furthest south of 64°58' in 1722, in a region where maps such as that of Ortelius (1570) showed an embayment, and he found an abundance of birds which seemed to indicate the proximity of land. The Frenchman Bouvet de Lozier discovered Bouvetøya (54°24'S), the most isolated island on earth, in 1739. He was not successful in sailing round it and so was able to maintain his conviction that it was part of an extensive coast.

Yves Joseph de Kerguelen-Tremarec was also searching for the continent when, in 1772, he came across the group of islands now known as the Kerguelen Islands at 49°30'S, again just about where Ortelius predicted a coastline. His faith in a temperate southern continent blinded him to the desolation of the islands, and he returned with glowing accounts of an inhabited and fertile land which he called 'La France Australe'. His story was believed and he was dispatched at the head of an expedition to colonize this new-found paradise. This time the bleak reality had to be admitted and on his return to France he was court-martialled, dismissed from the Navy, and imprisoned by the authorities who had been taken in by his salesmanship.

Writers went further in imaginative flights than the explorers. In the eighteenth century the South Pole had seemed as far away in human terms as Mars is today, and it was accepted as a place sufficiently remote and unknown to serve as a setting for fantasy. Robert Pultock, who must have been one of the very earliest writers of science fiction, published anonymously in 1751 *The Life and Adventures of Peter Wilkins, a Cornish Man: relating particularly to his shipwreck near the South Pole*. The story is about a race of vegetarian men and women, 'glumms' and 'gawreys', who could fly.

The only realistic features of the Antarctic scene were an exceptional magnetic deviation, icebergs, and the long darkness of winter. Interestingly, the glumms and gawreys carried dehydrated food on long flights – harking forward to sledge travel![5]

Nevertheless, the mirage of Terra Australis Incognita was eventually to lead to something real. When in 1768 the British Admiralty dispatched the *Endeavour* to the South Seas to observe the transit of Venus they chose as its leader not the Royal Society's nominee, Alexander Dalrymple, an able but somewhat foolish man obsessed with searching for the mythical continent of the map-makers, but a then comparatively unknown marine surveyor, James Cook. The scientific objective of the voyage was genuine – observation of the rare event of the planet Venus passing across the face of the sun would enable the earth's distance from the sun to be calculated – but Cook was also given secret instructions to search for a continent south of Tahiti. This search was a failure but otherwise the voyage, in the course of which New Zealand was circumnavigated and charted for the first time and the eastern coast of Australia discovered, was a resounding success. The Admiralty accepted without question Cook's suggestion of a second voyage to explore higher latitudes in the South, and in 1722 the *Resolution* and *Adventure* set sail from Plymouth on the voyage which was to be the beginning of Antarctic discovery.

Cook's plan was masterly. Making use of the prevailing winds and having Queen Charlotte's Sound in New Zealand as a harbour for refreshment, he was able to make three long sweeps to the south in the summer months, sailing around the world at a more southerly latitude than anyone else had ever done. Always getting as close to the ice as he could, he achieved his furthest south, at 71°10'S in the Pacific sector, on 30 January 1774. The *Resolution* was then perhaps only 160 kilometres (100 miles) or so from the Antarctic continent, the nearest it ever got, but visibility was not good and Cook and his officers saw nothing of land, nor did they ever claim definitely that they had. The ice at this point was so dense as to prevent further progress, but Cook was not disappointed:

> I who had Ambition not only to go farther than any one had done before, but as far as it was possible for man to go, was not sorry at meeting with this interruption as it in some measure relieved us, at least shortned the dangers and hardships inseparable with the Navigation of the Southern Polar Rigions: Sence therefore, we could not proceed one inch farther to the South, no other reason need be assigned for my Tacking and Standing back to the North.[6]

Although he never saw the continent, Cook had an intuitive feeling for the lie of the land, and it has proved to be of the general shape and extent that he predicted. His achievement in having cut the Terra Australis Incognita down to size and shown that the Southern Ocean was navigable was a tremendous one, but what he was proudest of, and what earned him the Royal Society's highest award – the Copley Medal – was his control of scurvy during the three-year voyage. The diet of sailors in those days was appalling – towards the end of a voyage the ship's biscuits were mouldy and full of weevils and the salt pork had to be towed behind the ship in a net for twenty-four hours before it could be faced as food – and, what was most important, deficient in vitamin C. After twelve to sixteen weeks of such a diet crews became enfeebled, lethargic, more liable to shipwreck, and eventually died. On another circumnavigation thirty years before Cook's, Anson lost over 1300 men from six ships' companies from this cause. Cook insisted on fresh vegetables whenever possible with regular consumption of such things as sauerkraut and, without being really sure what the effective item was, managed to provide his men with enough vitamin C to keep scurvy at bay. At the end of his account of the voyage Cook wrote:

It is with real satisfaction, and without claiming any merit but that of attention to my duty, that I can conclude this Account with an observation, which facts enable me to make, that our having discovered the possibility of preserving health amongst a numerous ship's company, for

The *Resolution* taking aboard ice, 9 January 1773; copper engraving after W. Hodges: 'We bore down to an island [iceberg] to leeward of us; there being about it some loose ice, part of which we saw break off. There we brought to; hoisted out three boats; and, in about five or six hours, took up as much ice as yielded fifteen tons of good fresh water.' (Cook, *A Voyage towards the South Pole*, 1777, vol. 1, p.37)

such a length of time, in such varieties of climate, and amidst such continued hardships and fatigues, will make this Voyage remarkable in the opinion of every benevolent person, when the disputes about a Southern Continent shall have ceased to engage the attention, and to divide the judgement of philosophers.[7]

He was modestly underestimating his contribution to geography, but it is certain that he could not have achieved what he did had he not the determination and perseverance to keep his crew healthy in spite of themselves. (He overcame their prejudice against fresh seal meat by decreeing that it should be served to officers only; before long there was a deputation from the seamen demanding that they should be treated equally.)

Cook lived at a time when the Romantic Movement and a consciousness of the sublime in the natural world were developing in Europe. Until then the more inhospitable features of nature, oceans and mountain ranges, had been largely regarded as nothing more than unproductive and dangerous obstacles to communication, to be avoided if at all possible. The poet Thomas Gray in 1739, then Jean-Jacques Rousseau in 1760, had been among the first to find a source of poetical inspiration and mystical exhilaration in mountain scenery. Later, the writings of Samuel Taylor Coleridge, the Wordsworths and a host of other nature writers were to establish a worship of the wilderness that persists undiminished today and finds one focus in Antarctica. Coleridge was taught mathematics by William Wales, who had been with Cook on his Antarctic voyage, and he is known to have consulted accounts of Cook's voyages among others when he was writing *The Rime of the Ancient Mariner*. The verse:

> And now there came both mist and snow,
> And it grew wondrous cold:
> And ice, mast-high, came floating by,
> As green as emerald.

strikes the authentic note. Gustave Doré, who later on illustrated *The Rime of the Ancient Mariner*, including a terrifyingly convincing portrayal of the loneliness and helplessness of a ship in a storm, did not do his homework so thoroughly and showed polar bears, animals which are not found in Antarctica, on an iceberg.[8] Cook, perhaps because he had been brought up amid the stern realities of life on a small farm beneath the Cleveland Hills, and although he was on familiar terms with the London intelligentsia before his Antarctic voyage, was in some respects of a prosaic cast of mind. If he saw any beauty in the Southern Ocean and its islands he did not confide this to his journals. Summing up on the Antarctic in 1775, towards the end of his

'And now the STORM-BLAST came, and he Was tyrannous and strong: He struck with his o'ertaking wings, And chased us south along.'

Wood engraving by Gustave Doré, illustrating *The Rime of the Ancient Mariner* by Samuel Taylor Coleridge, 1875.

voyage, he wrote of 'Lands doomed by Nature to everlasting frigidness and never to feel the warmth of the sun's rays, whose horrible and savage aspect I have not words to describe'.[9] The naturalist who was with him, Johann Reinhold Forster – a cantankerous character anyway – took an equally poor view, describing South Georgia as 'craggy, black and disgustful' and contrasting the 'horrid barrenness of the Southern Sandwich Land' with the 'gay enamel' of Tahiti.[10] In only one place in the Cook journals, in the entry for 24 February 1773, is there a hint that he was moved by the beauty of the Antarctic scene. That was when he conceded that 'the very curious and romantick Views'[6] which icebergs presented in some measure compensated for the nerve-racking business of sailing a ship through seas beset with them.

Cook's account of the Antarctic was thus not such as to encourage others to go there, but he – and, perhaps more to the point, his crew – had seen fur seals in large numbers. Fur seal skins could be sold for fantastic prices in the market in Canton, China, and following Cook's voyage, sealing quickly spread from the tip of South America and the Falkland Islands, where it was already going on, to South Georgia and then to other islands in the Southern Ocean. The slaughter was prodigious; if it could be done, every seal on a beach was killed and its skin taken. A few sealers felt qualms; an officer on a sealing ship wrote: 'what murder is committed merely for the divesting of the animal, for the gratification of our pride'.[11] Some realized that there would soon be no seals left anywhere, but for a time there was faith in the existence of sealing grounds yet undiscovered. Of course, if he did find new grounds it was not in a sealer's interests to let anyone else know where they were. Sealers' log books are usually distressingly short on details, providing endless scope now for arguments about priority of discovery, but the lure of quick profits and a spirit of adventure led one sealer after another to explore the Antarctic islands – the South Shetlands, Macquarie Island, the South Orkneys and the Balleny Islands – and then the tip of the Antarctic Peninsula and the continent itself.

It is now generally accepted that it was Captain William Smith with the Royal Navy's ship's master Edward Bransfield in the brig *Williams* who made the first recorded sighting of the rocks of Trinity Land, the northernmost part of the Antarctic Peninsula and opposite South America, on 30 January 1820. Bransfield drew a chart of his discovery which still exists. Nathaniel Palmer, an American sealer aged only twenty-one, made a similar sighting from the shallop *Hero* in November of the same year. The first man known actually to have landed on the Antarctic mainland was another American sealing captain, John Davis, in the shallop *Cecilia*. This was on 7 February 1821 and the spot was probably in Hughes Bay, on the west coast of the Peninsula, about 240 kilometres (150 miles) from its tip.

The life of a sealer was one of discomfort, privation, ever-present danger

Charity Glacier, Livingston Island (oil)

and carnage, and the region in which they had to work is one of the cloudiest and stormiest in the world. Often a sealing gang would be landed on an island to be picked up months or even years later, and until then to live a life devoid of all comfort, fending as best they could with seal meat to eat and blubber for fuel. The occasional calm sunny day, when the mountains and snow fields could be seen and ice displayed its blues and greens against a deep blue sea, must have lifted his spirits, but the average sealer was not one to say so. A few sealing captains, however, were handy with their pens. Such was James Weddell, the son of a Lanarkshire upholsterer living in London, who in the brig *Jane* accompanied by the even smaller cutter *Beaufoy* went further south than Cook had done, creating a record for penetration of the Weddell Sea that was not to be surpassed for nearly ninety years. Another was Captain Edmund Fanning, a native of Stonington, Connecticut, USA, who commanded several vessels on sealing expeditions in the Southern Ocean. These were both educated, well-read men who made acute observations on the Antarctic and its wildlife which they put into books about their voyages. Weddell's account is in spare, clear English but with no indications of his appreciation or otherwise of the Antarctic scene.[12] He made sketches of some of the lands and objects he saw, but these, in their final engraved form, are dull. Fanning's literary style is more laboured, but he did express his enjoyment of the scenery of South Georgia:

> The surgeon and myself had strolled, or rather climbed, to an elevated precipice of the mountain; from this position a wide and extensive view of the ocean was had, covered with fleets of immense ice-islands. The brightness of a clear sun shining on these islands, and on the sea as it broke against their base, formed a view, which for grandeur and beauty, is seldom or ever surpassed.[13]

There was perhaps even more danger in the more frequented seas than in the Southern Ocean in those days, and Fanning had exciting adventures with pirates on returning from delivering his seal skins in Canton. Fanning helped to organize the first United States exploring expedition to the Antarctic. This was not altogether successful but it did result in some excellent studies of the geology and zoology of the South Shetlands. These were the work of James Eights who emerged from obscurity with the half-dozen or so scientific papers he wrote on his Antarctic work, only to return to it again for the rest of his long life. It is suggested that blighted love was the cause of his failure to live up to his early promise. He was something of an artist, having produced a popular series of colour pictures of his native town, Albany, as well as some fine zoological drawings, and was appreciative of the beauties of the South Shetland scene:

The sky too in these latitudes presents a very singular aspect; being most generally filled with innumerable clouds, torn into ragged and irregular patches by the wild gales which every where race over the Antarctic seas: the sun as it rises or sets, slowly and obliquely in the southern horizon, sends its rays through the many openings between, tinging them here and there with every variety of hue and colour, from whence they are thrown in mild and beautiful reflections upon the extensive fields of snow which lie piled on the surrounding hills, giving to the whole scene for a greater part of the long summer day, the ever varying effect of a most gorgeous sunset.[14]

The fur rush in the Antarctic ended as suddenly as it had begun. By 1829, it was said, there was not a fur seal to be seen in the South Shetlands. But before then some governments were realizing that they ought to know more of this remote part of the world, even if nothing more useful were to come of it than knowledge of how to navigate its waters and get there if someone else were to discover something desirable. Tsar Alexander I, in a fit of enthusiasm, took the advice of his naval experts that a sea route via the far south might be the best means of getting to his eastern province of Kamchatka, and in 1819 dispatched Thaddeus Bellingshausen on a circumnavigation in the Southern Ocean.

Bellingshausen was a superb seaman. He kept the two ill-matched vessels of his expedition, the fast-sailing *Vostok* and the much slower *Mirnyi*,

The Russian expedition in the Antarctic, 1819–21. (Courtesy of the Scott Polar Research Institute)

Icescape (water-colour)

together in a voyage which circled Antarctica at high latitudes and cleverly complemented, rather than overlapped, that of Cook. Bellingshausen was the first to sight the Antarctic continent, that is, if, as seems reasonable, it is allowed that fast-ice (ice attached to the land) is part of the continent. From his navigation charts, which, unlike his logs and other original manuscripts, have survived, it is clear that he sighted the seaward edge of the continental ice shelf at 69°37'S off the Princess Martha Coast between 16 and 17 January 1820. This was three days before William Smith and Edward Bransfield sighted Trinity Land.[15] Later in the voyage, Bellingshausen discovered Peter I Island, the first land to be found within the Antarctic Circle, and Alexander Land, now known to be an island.

There was an enigmatic encounter between Thaddeus Bellingshausen and Nathaniel Palmer off the South Shetlands as the *Vostok* and *Mirnyi* turned north for home. Bellingshausen described this meeting rather laconically in his account of his voyage[16], mainly concerning himself with statistics of the seal industry supplied by Palmer. Palmer left no written record, but his verbal accounts seem to have acquired more details as the years went by. As told twenty-three years after the event it appears that, while the *Hero* was becalmed in thick fog, Palmer was astounded to get an answer when he struck the ship's bell. When the mist cleared he found himself between two warships which, in reply to his raising the American flag, ran up the Russian colours. Palmer went aboard the *Vostok* and was invited to lunch. When he heard of Palmer's sighting of the continent, Bellingshausen is reported as having said, in a downcast manner: 'What shall I say to my master? What will he think of me? But, be that as it may, my grief is your joy. Wear your laurels. With my sincere prayers for your welfare, I name the land you discovered in honor of yourself, noble boy, Palmer's Land.'[17] Perhaps so, or more probably the Tsar's attention was taken up with other things, but Bellingshausen's return was greeted with no great enthusiasm and, although he ended his days as Admiral and Governor of the port of Kronshtadt, it took special pleading to get his account of the voyage published, and even then it attracted little notice. Now we can recognize his as an achievement second only to that of Cook.

The attention of sealers became diverted from the fur seal to the elephant seal, which yielded a good quality oil, but this was less profitable. Ever hopeful, sealing captains continued their search for new grounds, but some of this exploration was now done for its own sake without much expectation of immediate financial returns. The British firm of Enderby Brothers was outstanding in this. Originally it had been engaged in trade across the North Atlantic but, after an upsetting experience at Boston in 1773 when delivering a cargo of tea, had switched to sealing and whaling in southern seas. Samuel Enderby, the founder of the firm, had been interested in hearing about the out-of-the-way places his ships visited and this trait was more strongly developed in one of his three sons, Charles, who became a founder member of the Royal Geographical Society in 1830. As captains for their vessels, the Enderbys liked to have men with some education and naval experience and encouraged them in exploration. This led to a succession of notable exploits and discoveries in the Antarctic and, eventually, to the ruination of the business. John Biscoe in the brig *Tula* accompanied by the cutter *Lively*, of only 150 and 50 tonnes respectively, circumnavigated the continent in 1830–2 at latitudes which were sometimes even further south than those of Bellingshausen. He sighted a coast in the Indian Ocean sector which he called Enderby Land and which he was convinced was part of a large continent. During this part of his voyage there were auroral displays; his journal records:

> Nearly the whole night, the Aurora Australis showed the most brilliant appearance, at times rolling itself over our heads in beautiful columns, then as suddenly forming itself as the unrolled fringe of a curtain, and again suddenly shooting to the form of a serpent, and at times appearing not many yards above us . . . At this time we were completely beset with broken ice, and although the vessels were in considerable danger in running through it with a smart breeze, which had now sprung up, I could hardly restrain the people from looking at the Aurora Australis instead of the vessel's course.[18]

After a pause in Tasmania, he went on round to the west coast of the Antarctic Peninsula, where he discovered a large island which he named in honour of Queen Adelaide. It was a brilliant voyage of exploration, but a failure as far as sealing was concerned, and it finished with Biscoe losing many of his crew from scurvy, the desertion of nearly all the others and the shipwreck of the *Lively*. He was awarded a Royal Premium, the equivalent of a gold medal, by the Royal Geographical Society but died in poverty eleven years later. Peter Kemp, also, probably, an Enderby captain, sailing the *Magnet*, sighted Heard Island (which was rediscovered by Captain Heard of the American vessel *Oriental* in 1853) and the Kemp Coast in the Indian Ocean sector in 1833–4. Two more Enderby vessels, the cutter *Sabrina* and the schooner *Eliza Scott*, commanded respectively by H. Freeman and John Balleny, explored south from New Zealand in 1838–9. They discovered the Balleny Islands, on which a hazardous and fleeting landing was made, and sighted the Sabrina Coast. The *Sabrina* was lost without trace shortly afterwards, but the *Eliza Scott* got safely back to London in time to pass on the information gained to the naval expedition which was about to depart under Ross's command.[18] In this period, it might be noted, the interest of whalers in the Antarctic was slight; whales were still abundant nearer to home and the big whales of the far south were far more difficult to handle than the amenable 'right' whale of temperate waters.

Thus, in the late 1830s, there was little of commercial interest to induce governments to support Antarctic exploration. However, scientists were much preoccupied with the earth's magnetic properties at that time and could argue that it was of great importance for navigation that more should be known about the magnetic field in the far south. The German physicist Gauss had put forward a theory from which the position of the South Magnetic Pole and the lines of force around it could be predicted, but sailors obviously preferred established fact to theory. There was also much prestige to be gained from successful geographical exploration.

It was thoughts of this sort that led King Louis-Philippe of France to send Captain Jules Sébastien-César Dumont d'Urville, who had previously distinguished himself by acquiring the Venus de Milo for France, on an expedition south with the ships *Astrolabe* and *Zelée*. The King offered to the officers and crew a reward from the privy purse for every degree passed after 67° and 'whatever you choose to ask for' if the Pole itself were reached. Luckily for him, the King was not called on to fulfil the latter part of his promise.

OPPOSITE The *Astrolabe* taking aboard ice, 6 February 1838. Lithograph after L. le Breton. (d'Urville, *Atlas Pittoresque*, 1841–5, vol. 1, plate 22: courtesy of the Scott Polar Research Institute)

BELOW The corvettes *Astrolabe* and *Zelée* in the pack-ice of the Weddell Sea, 6 February 1838. Lithograph after E. Goupil. (d'Urville, *Atlas Pittoresque*, 1841–5, vol. 1, plate 20: courtesy of the Scott Polar Research Institute)

D'Urville's heart was really in ethnographic research in the South Sea islands and he had not bargained for a royal command to go to the South Pole when he petitioned the government for support for a voyage of exploration. In 1837, when he sailed from Toulon, he was nearing fifty and ill with gout. Hobbling up the gangplank, he overheard a sailor remark: *'Oh! ce bonhomme-là ne nous mènera pas bien loin!* ('That old chap won't take us very far!'), and perhaps this nettled him into determined efforts to carry out his orders. He made a brave attempt, in what were unsuitable ships for ice navigation, to follow Weddell's track south, but it was a bad year and he had to abandon the idea after a terrifying five days in the pack.

This might have satisfied honour, but towards the end of his circum-navigation, hearing of American and British plans to reach the South Magnetic Pole, he decided to go beyond his instructions and secure this glory for France. Sailing south from Tasmania, he sighted the Antarctic continent in January 1840. To reach the Magnetic Pole was obviously impossible since it was well inland, but a landing was made and *'Suivant l'ancienne coutume que les Anglais ont conservée précieusement, nous en prîmes possession au nom de la France.'* ('Following the venerable custom which the English have

Crossing the Polar Circle aboard the *Astrolabe*, 20 January 1840. Lithograph after L. le Breton. (d'Urville, *Atlas Pittoresque*, 1841–5, vol. 2, plate 167: courtesy of the Scott Polar Research Institute)

Strong gale in the ice off Adélie Land. Lithograph after L. le Breton. (d'Urville, *Atlas Pittoresque*, 1841–5, vol. 2, plate 172: courtesy of the Scott Polar Research Institute)

carefully maintained, we took possession in the name of France.') A toast was drunk – '*Jamais vin de Bordeaux ne fut appelé à jouer un rôle plus digne*' ('Never had the wine of Bordeaux been called upon to play a more worthy part') – and he named the land, in honour of his wife, Terre Adélie.[19] He also named the adelie penguin after her. This was surely meant as a compliment, but some who have studied this bird more closely describe it variously as thieving, quarrelsome, belligerent, filthy and stupid.

A few days after this landing, the *Astrolabe* was making a south-westerly course through high seas at 68°48'S when an amazed lookout saw a ship coming from the east and closing fast. What happened is unclear, except that there was misunderstanding on both sides, but the two vessels passed within hailing distance with no greeting exchanged and no communication attempted.

The ship from the east was the *Porpoise* of the United States Exploring Expedition under the command of Lieutenant Charles Wilkes USN. This expedition of six vessels, including the sloop-of-war *Vincennes* as flagship, had set sail from Norfolk, Virginia, in 1838 after a period of thoroughly democratic bickering and vacillation. His fleet was not only ill-suited for navigation in the Antarctic but ill-assorted and shoddily fitted out, as Wilkes fully realized. However, he was a man of great courage and determination, resolved that the expedition should be a credit to the United States.

His first venture into Antarctic waters, in the Peninsula region, was late in the season and achieved little that was particularly noteworthy. His second venture south, from Sydney, Australia, in the austral summer of 1839–40, was much more successful. A stretch of coast about 2400 kilometres (1500 miles) long was charted. In making his survey, Wilkes did not take polar mirage into account so that distances were underestimated and later explorers, including Ross the following year, took an unkind delight in sailing over Wilkes Land. Nevertheless Wilkes had, without question, established the existence of a new, considerable, and continuous coastline, thereby showing for the first time that there is an Antarctic continent.

Altogether the voyage took four years and explored many parts of the world apart from the Antarctic, bringing back a magnificent harvest of

Landing from the *Astrolabe* and *Zelée* on Adélie Land, 21 January 1840. Lithograph after L. le Breton. (d'Urville, *Atlas Pittoresque*, 1841–5, vol. 2, plate 170: courtesy of the Scott Polar Research Institute)

natural history and ethnographic specimens.[20] Sadly, the return of the expedition was greeted with indifference – and Wilkes's own officers, resentful of his high-handedness, laid charges which resulted in his court martial. Happily, he was acquitted and later rose to high rank in the US Navy. His determination in the conduct of the expedition extended to seeing that its results were published and eventually, after much trouble, the outcome was worthy – a five-volume *Narrative* and twenty volumes of scientific reports.[21]

At about the same time, the British government sent the ships *Erebus* and *Terror* under Captain James Clark Ross RN to conduct a magnetic survey in southern waters. This expedition was prepared with thoroughness and showed Victorian England at its best. The two ships were of the type known as 'bombs', immensely strong wooden vessels well suited for working through ice. They succeeded in penetrating the pack just south of New Zealand into the open waters of what is now called the Ross Sea. Here, the Antarctic continent, hitherto glimpsed partially and at a distance, was at last seen by human eye in its full magnificence. Ross found along the coast a stupendous range of snow-covered peaks, two huge volcanoes – one of them spectacularly active – whales and penguins in their hundreds and thousands,

The *Vincennes*, flagship of the US Exploring Expedition 1838–42, anchored near an 'ice-island' off Wilkes Land. Engraving after a sketch by Charles Wilkes. (Wilkes, *Narrative of the US Exploring Expedition 1844*, vol. 2, p.325: courtesy of the Scott Polar Research Institute)

and, most amazing of all, a completely new thing, a level barrier of ice, 60 metres (200 feet) high, stretching for hundreds of miles across their path south. All this was seen, on some days at least, under a clear blue sky and brilliant sun.

There was elation over what was clearly a major geographic discovery but also, from the captain to the ordinary seaman, a feeling of having seen the sublime. In his account of the voyage Ross wrote as follows:

> Early this morning we had a fine view of the magnificent chain of mountains that we had seen stretching away to the southward some days before, but then more imperfectly. With a moderate southerly wind we had beautifully clear weather, and we now saw them to great advantage; and as we stood towards them, we gazed with feelings of indescribable delight upon a scene of grandeur and magnificence far beyond anything we had before seen or could have conceived. These mountains also were completely covered to their sharply-pointed summits with snow, and the elevation[s] that were measured roughly, varied from twelve to upwards of fourteen thousand feet. These were named after the eminent philosophers of the Royal Society and British Association, at whose recommendation the government was induced to send forth this expedition.[22]

Mount Sabine and Possession Island, discovered 11 January 1841. Lithograph after J. E. Davis. (Ross, *A Voyage of Discovery and Research in the Southern and Antarctic Regions*, 1847, vol. 1, p.183: courtesy of the Scott Polar Research Institute)

His surgeon, Robert McCormick, found it difficult not to remain on deck, sketching the panorama as it unfolded, at all hours of day and night. McCormick's assistant, Joseph Dalton Hooker, later to become Director of the Royal Botanic Gardens, Kew, and one of the most distinguished scientists of his time, confined himself in his journal to matters of fact, although he made vivid little sketches of icebergs, scenery, and events such as seamen rounding up emperor penguins. Eminent Victorian though he was to be, Hooker let his hair down on occasion; J. E. Davis, the second master of the *Terror*, told of some New Year revels in a letter to his sister:

> I dined on board the Erebus and after dinner, Hooker (the Assistant Surgeon of the Erebus) and myself went on the ice and cut out in hard snow the figure of a woman which we called our 'Venus de Medici' – she was made sitting down and about 8 feet long and as the snow froze very hard she remained perfect till we left the floe.[23]

It is a pity that d'Urville had already moved on from those parts and was not there to find it.

Hooker, in commenting on the expedition's equipment, mentioned that 'no instrument, however newly invented, was omitted, even down to an apparatus for "daguerrotyping and talbotyping"'. How to carry out the latter

Beaufort Island and Mount Erebus, discovered 28 January 1841. Lithograph after J. E. Davis. (Ross, *A Voyage of Discovery and Research in the Southern and Antarctic Regions*, 1847, vol. 1, p.216: courtesy of the Scott Polar Research Institute)

of these photographic processes had only been disclosed by Fox Talbot six months before the expedition sailed and it seems that neither was used to any purpose, which was sad – there might have been some really historic photographs. When lecturing after his return, Hooker enthused about the beauty of the scenery:

> The water and the sky were both as blue, or rather more intensely blue, than I have ever seen them in the tropics, and all the coast one sparkling mass, which when the sun approached the horizon, reflected the most brilliant tints of golden yellow and scarlet. Then to see the dark cloud of smoke tinged with broad sheets of flame rising in an unbroken column from the volcano, one side jet black, the other giving off various-coloured fire, and sometimes turning to seaward and stretching many miles along the strata of the upper air. This was a sight so surpassing everything that can be conceived and so heightened by the consciousness that we had penetrated into regions far beyond what had been deemed practicable before, that it caused a feeling of awe to steal over us at the contemplation of our comparatively utter insignificance and helplessness, and at the same time an indescribable and lively conviction of the greatness of the Creator in these works of his hand.[24]

James Savage, blacksmith and armourer aboard Captain Ross's ship, the

Seal-hunting on the pack-ice. Woodcut after a sketch by Joseph Hooker. (Ross, *A Voyage of Discovery and Research in the Southern and Antarctic Regions*, 1847, vol. 2, p.33: courtesy of the Scott Polar Research Institute)

Erebus, dictated his account to a mess-mate, C. J. Sullivan:

> On the morning of the Eight D° [February 1841] we found our Selves Enclosed in a beautiful bay of the barrier. All hands when the[y] Came on Deck to view this the most rare and magnificent Sight that Ever the human Eye witness[d] Since the world was created actually Stood Motionless for Several Seconds before he Could Speak to the next man to him.
>
> Beholding with Silent Surprize the great and wonderful works of nature in this position we had an opportunity to discern the barrier in its Splendid position. Then i wish[d] i was an artist or a draughtsman instead of a blacksmith and Armourer We Set a Side all thought of mount Erebus and Victoria's Land to bear in mind the more Immaginative thoughts of this rare Phenomena that was lost to human view
>
>   In Gone by Ages
>
> When Cap[tn] Ross Came on deck he was Equally Surpriz[d] to See the Beautiful Sight Though being in the north Arctic Regions one half his life he never see any ice in Arctic Seas to be compar[d] to the Barrier.[25]

New Year's Day 1842 on the ice. Water-colour by J. E. Davis. (Courtesy of the Scott Polar Research Institute)

Sullivan had poetic leanings and, when the *Erebus* later sailed over a spot where Wilkes had reported land, he burst into chauvinistic verse:

> Like the Lying yankey who made his boast
> he Saw high land & reached no Coast
> when we returned from Seventy Eight
> a hundred miles Each way we beat
> But Low the land the yankeys See
> was Sunk and Gone neath the Sea.

The voyages of d'Urville, Wilkes and Ross were accomplished without loss of ships or lives while in Antarctic waters. When one thinks that these were sailing vessels which had to be handled in the stormiest seas in the world, often in thick fog, hemmed in by pack-ice and icebergs, and the crew benumbed by cold, one can only marvel at the superlative seamanship. Ross described one storm thus:

> Although we had been forced many miles deeper into the pack, we could not perceive that the swell had at all subsided, our ships still rolling and groaning amidst the heavy fragments of crushing bergs, over which the ocean rolled its mountainous waves, throwing huge masses one upon another, and then again burying them deep beneath its foaming waters, dashing and grinding them together with fearful violence. The awful grandeur of such a scene can neither be imagined nor described, far less can the feelings of those who witnessed it be understood. Each of us secured our hold, waiting the issue with resignation to the will of Him who alone could preserve us, and bring us safely through this extreme danger; watching with breathless anxiety the effect of each succeeding collision, and the vibrations of the tottering masts, expecting every moment to see them give way without our having the power to make an effort to save them.[26]

No other vessels of the time could have survived such battering, but the worst that happened to the *Erebus* and *Terror* was that their rudders were damaged. On another occasion, the *Erebus*, running before the wind, encountered a large berg which suddenly appeared out of the falling snow and was run down by the *Terror* as she altered course to avoid it. The *Erebus* was completely disabled and only saved from being wrecked in collision with the berg by the hazardous expedient of a 'sternboard' – that is, going astern with reversed helm when the bows, if all goes well, should continue to swing in the direction of the ship's original turn.

After these three splendid voyages there followed what has become known as the 'age of averted interest'. For the next thirty years there were no major expeditions to the Antarctic and only two in the twenty years after that. There were various reasons for this. There were no commercial incentives – whales were still abundant in the north – and colonization was pointless. Enough was known about the earth's magnetic field to suffice for the time being. Indeed there was little interest on the part of scientists. It is clear from the writings of men such as Ross and Hooker, who had been there, that they saw nothing of compelling scientific importance about the continent and that they thought it unlikely that scientists would again visit such an inaccessible place. The philosophy of science at that time was overwhelmingly 'reductionist', that is to say, concerned with individual things and processes. This approach was having spectacular success in electricity and chemistry and the opposite, holistic, philosophy of viewing systems, including the natural world, as integrated wholes, was out of fashion. The solitary voice of the distinguished American oceanographer and meteorologist Matthew Maury, pointing out that it was impossible to understand ocean currents or the weather of the southern hemisphere without knowing what was going on in Antarctica, was insufficient to persuade governments that they ought to spend money on Antarctic investigations.

Nevertheless, slowly, Antarctica began to find a place in public consciousness. Words are inadequate to convey the Antarctic scene, and the gripping passages of most accounts of Antarctic exploration in this early period are embedded in masses of daily reports of weather, sea conditions and

Collision between the *Erebus* and the *Terror* to the windward of a chain of icebergs, 13 March 1842. Lithograph after J. E. Davis. (Ross, *A Voyage of Discovery and Research in the Southern and Antarctic Regions*, 1847, vol. 2, frontispiece: courtesy of the Scott Polar Research Institute)

Tabular iceberg, Weddell Sea (oil)

navigational details. D'Urville's *Voyage au Pole Sud*[19] is one of the best; indeed, his vivid descriptions of the Antarctic have been considered of more worth than his actual geographic discoveries. Of course, artists went on the early voyages of exploration for the very practical purpose of recording what was seen. Cook took with him the landscape painter William Hodges and d'Urville's report was illustrated with some particularly fine plates. Although the artist he took with him, Ernest-Auguste Goupil, died at Hobart before the principal Antarctic leg of the voyage, it fortunately happened that an assistant surgeon, Louis le Breton, showed remarkable talent in illustration. There was enough in print or picture to serve as a basis for a few works of imaginative literature. Edgar Allen Poe wrote two romances placed in Antarctica; *MS Found in a Bottle* (1833) described a voyage undertaken out of curiosity which ended in horror as the narrator with his ship was sucked into a gigantic whirlpool amid the ice, and *Narrative of A. Gordon Pym* (1838), another horror story, harked back to Weddell's theory that open sea surrounded the South Pole. The latter work of Poe's is supposed to have been one inspiration for Hermann Melville, who himself had sailed the south seas, when he wrote *Moby Dick* (1851). About the same time, Fenimore

HMS *Challenger* firing at an iceberg. (B. Shephard's *Sketchbook of the HMS Challenger Expedition 1872–1874*, ed. Stewart & Henderson, 1972, p.33: courtesy of the Scott Polar Research Institute)

The *Challenger* in Christmas Harbour, Kerguelen. (Wild, *At Anchor*, 1878: courtesy of the Scott Polar Research Institute)

Cooper wrote a sea story, *The Sea Lions* (1848), using Wilkes's narrative as a source of descriptions of the Southern Ocean and its icebergs and pack ice. Poe's *Narrative of A. Gordon Pym* was followed up by Jules Verne in his *Le sphinx des glaces*, published in translation in 1899 as *An Antarctic Mystery*. It is not one of his best stories.

Of the two noteworthy voyages to the Antarctic which were carried out before interest really revived, that of HMS *Challenger* in 1872–6 was primarily for a world-wide oceanographic study. She was the first steamship to cross the Antarctic Circle, but did not get within sight of the continent. Icebergs were encountered – too closely on one occasion – and the first of what by now must be many tens of thousands of photographs of them were taken. Perhaps the *Challenger's* greatest contribution to knowledge of the Antarctic was the finding that rocks brought up by dredging from the bottom of the Southern Ocean, and evidently dropped there by melting icebergs, were of continental character. This confirmed that there really was a continent there. The other voyage was of the *Grönland*, sent out by the German Society for Polar Navigation and commanded by Captain Eduard Dallman. The *Grönland* carried out sealing and exploration in the South Shetland Islands and along the west coast of the Antarctic Peninsula. This was in an area previously visited by Biscoe, but Dallman went further and found Bismark Strait where Biscoe had supposed there was land.[27]

Ice-floes and Brunt Ice Shelf (water-colour)

Chapter Two

Exploration of the Continent

I NTEREST in the Antarctic revived for good and not-so-good reasons. On the one hand, scientists began to feel that they were shamefully ignorant of this substantial part of the earth's surface. It was being realized that some problems could only be tackled by making simultaneous (synoptic) measurements from different points on the surface of the earth. The First International Polar Year, held in 1882–3, gave expression to this in a programme of synoptic observations of magnetism and weather. It was concentrated on the Arctic with only one site, on South Georgia, representing the Antarctic, but it showed its value by giving for the first time a detailed picture on a global scale of the vagaries of terrestrial magnetism. Leading geographers such as Sir Clements Markham in Britain and Professor Georg von Neumayer in Germany campaigned for renewed exploration and this resulted in the Sixth International Geographical Congress held in London in 1895, resolving that 'The exploration of the Antarctic regions is the greatest piece of geographical exploration still to be undertaken' and that efforts should be made to fill this gap 'before the close of the century.'

With less worthy motives, whalers were also looking south. Stocks in the northern hemisphere were becoming exhausted and the recent invention of the explosive-headed harpoon propelled from a cannon allowed them to think of taking the big blue and fin whales that were so abundant in the Southern Ocean. There were four expeditions in the 1890s to assess the situation. One from Dundee consisted of four vessels, *Balaena*, *Active*, *Diana* and *Polar Star*, and went to the Peninsula area. The Norwegian schooner *Jason* under the command of Captain C. A. Larsen, who was to become the big name in Antarctic whaling, visited this same area twice. The *Antarctic* expedition led by Captain L. Kristensen and H. J. Bull went to the Ross Sea. Little in the way of whale oil or geographical discovery came out of these ventures and the naturalist W. S. Bruce returned from the Dundee expedition utterly frustrated. However, on Seymour Island Larsen found fossils which showed that Antarctica once enjoyed a more congenial climate, and Bull collected lichens, the first plants to be found as far south as 72°S. Perhaps the most important outcome was that the *Antarctic* expedition showed that it was not too difficult to penetrate into the Ross Sea and to land at a site which seemed suitable for overwintering.

The scientists were slower in getting things moving, mainly because they found it more difficult to raise funds, partly because they needed more time to plan, and to some extent because they quarrelled amongst themselves[28]. The first two expeditions to get away were both the result of individual enterprise and private funding. One was that in the *Belgica* in 1898–9, captained by Adrien de Gerlache, which became the first expedition to overwinter in the Antarctic and which foreshadowed the international character of later Antarctic endeavour. It was funded from Belgium, but the *Belgica* was of Norwegian build and her company included, besides Belgians, a Rumanian, a Pole, several Norwegians, a Russian and an American. One of the Norwegians was Roald Amundsen, later to be first at the South Pole, and the American was Frederick A. Cook, who subsequently made a claim, which was disputed, to have reached the North Pole. It is not clear whether Gerlache deliberately got his ship beset, but she did become frozen in, to the west of the Antarctic Peninsula. After a harrowing winter during which one man died, another went mad and all were affected mentally to some degree, the *Belgica* was released after having drifted with the ice through almost 17° of longitude.[29]

An expedition in 1898–1900, sponsored by the British newspaper magnate Sir George Newnes, and led by the Norwegian Karsten Borchgrevink, who had been with Bull on the *Antarctic* expedition, was the first to overwinter on land, at Cape Adare at the western end of the Ross Sea. They too had a bad time; their huts narrowly escaped being burnt down and one member of the expedition died.[30] Borchgrevink was regarded as an outsider by the British establishment, who considered that he had obtained funds which they might have had for their expedition, and his achievements were recognized only slowly. He was the first to obtain detailed records of the climate of the maritime Antarctic, and he reached 78°50′S, the furthest south so far.

Three big national expeditions set off in 1901. There was some consultation between the expeditions, at least to the extent of ensuring they did not overlap. The British went to the Ross Sea area, the Germans to Enderby Land

and the Swedes to the east coast of the Peninsula.

The British National Antarctic Expedition, Scott's first expedition, from 1901 to 1904 in the *Discovery*, was in some respects amateurish but it did important scientific work in the Ross Sea area, made a long journey towards the Pole, sighted a long stretch of the magnificent Transantarctic Mountains, reached the polar plateau for the first time, and discovered Taylor Valley – the first example of the remarkable snow- and ice-free areas which provide the nearest approach on earth to the conditions which exist on the surface of Mars.[31]

The German expedition under Erich von Drygalski sailed in the *Gauss* and, after sighting the continent to the south-east of Kerguelen, was promptly entrapped by the ice. The winter was fully taken up with scientific observations and sledge journeys to the adjacent land. Like Scott, Drygalski used a balloon to survey the terrain but he went one further in technical innovation by recording penguin noises on an Edison phonograph. There was anxiety in the spring when blasting and sawing failed to set the *Gauss* free, but Drygalski solved the problem by laying a trail of rubbish over the 600 metres (2000 feet) to the open water. The dark-coloured gash absorbed the heat of the sun and a channel was eventually melted, through which the ship escaped to reach the Fatherland safely by November 1903. The Kaiser was disappointed that so little new territory had been discovered, but twenty massive volumes of scientific results were published.[32]

The Swedish expedition in the *Antarctic*, that same ship which was only the second to visit the Ross Sea, was led by Otto Nordenskjöld with C. A. Larsen, the whaler, as his captain. There was thus no shortage of experience, but this expedition too was beset, and with a less happy outcome. After Nordenskjöld and five companions had been left on Snow Hill Island, the ship went back north to the Falklands. When she attempted to return the following year to pick up the wintering party, the way was blocked with ice so three men were dispatched on foot to establish contact with Nordenskjöld. They lost their way and had to return to their depot at Hope Bay where they overwintered in a makeshift hut, living mainly on penguins. Meanwhile, Larsen had attempted to force a passage but the *Antarctic* was caught, crushed, and sank, those aboard managing to reach Paulet Island where they spent a terrible winter.

The story is a complicated and dramatic one and cannot be told here in the detail it deserves, but the Hope Bay trio managed to get to Snow Hill Island the following season and, by an incredible but nevertheless true coincidence, about a month later on the same day so did an Argentinian rescue expedition and Larsen's party from Paulet Island. No lives had been lost. Valuable material went down with the *Antarctic* but nevertheless the scientific contribution of the expedition was a substantial one.[33]

Other expeditions to the Peninsula area followed. There was a Scottish expedition under Bruce – who was determined to do some science this time. His ship, the *Scotia*, penetrated into the Weddell Sea, discovering Coats Land and adding much to knowledge of the hydrography of that part of the Southern Ocean. The South Orkney Islands, which had scarcely been visited

The piper and the penguin, an encounter during the *Scotia*'s visit to Coats Land, March 1904. (Rudmose Brown, *A Naturalist at the Poles*, 1923, p.112)

since they were discovered by the sealer Captain Powell in 1821, were explored and a meteorological station was established on Laurie Island, one of the group. When the expedition was over, Bruce suggested that the British government should operate it on a permanent basis. This offer was refused so Bruce handed it over to Argentina, which has occupied it continuously ever since. The words in the account of the voyage were prescient:

> The Argentine naval flag was hoisted on the cairn where formerly the Scottish Lion flew; and I presume the South Orkneys are looked on as a possession of that power, – the nucleus of an empire, perhaps, they may even seem to ambitious Argentine expansionists.[34]

In those days it was considered necessary to devote three pages of the account to explaining to British readers what skiing was. One of the most famous pictures in the book is of a kilted piper playing to an emperor penguin; the text recorded that the birds were indifferent to bagpipe music but inspection of some versions of this photograph shows that the bird had to be tethered in position. In 1903–5 in the *Français*, and again in 1908–10 in the *Pourquoi-Pas?*, Dr Jean-Baptiste Charcot explored the west coast of the Peninsula, producing some excellent charts and a substantial patch of French names on the map.[35]

Ernest Shackleton, who had been with Scott on his pioneering journey south across the ice shelf, had been invalided home from the *Discovery* expedition. This rankled and he organized his own, which sailed in the *Nimrod* in 1907. He had agreed with Scott not to trespass in the McMurdo Sound area, which Scott regarded as his, but circumstances forced Shackleton's hand and he had to set up his base at Cape Royds on Ross Island, only some 30 kilometres (20 miles) from Hut Point where the *Discovery* had wintered. Among his men were Douglas Mawson and Raymond Priestley, both of whom were to achieve fame both as Antarctic explorers and scientists, and a gentle fifty-year-old Professor of Geology, Edgeworth David FRS, who was to prove tough enough to undertake the most arduous journeys. Mount Erebus was climbed and the South Magnetic Pole attained, both for the first time, but the outstanding achievement was a journey starting along Scott's track across the Ross Ice Shelf, up the Beardmore Glacier (once thought to be the largest in the world), and on to the polar plateau to within 97 nautical miles of the South Pole itself. In many ways this must be reckoned as the greatest of all polar journeys – the crucial decision to turn back when so tantalizingly near the ultimate goal must have been agonizing, but it was the right one if the party was to survive to tell the tale.

As it was, they only just survived, and it was by no means in a spirit of amity and mutual trust. Shackleton's diary, written with the public in mind, was generous to his three companions but they were less restrained. Frank

Wild kept a diary in which he vituperated in code about the others and the Antarctic in general. Eric Marshall was particularly scathing about Shackleton, describing him among other things as an old woman and a hopeless cook. Nevertheless, in Wild's case the magic of the Antarctic re-asserted itself and, vowing he would ne'er return, he did so, again with Shackleton. It was he who kept the survivors of the British Imperial Trans-Antarctic Expedition alive and sane on Elephant Island – an experience quite as horrible as the furthest south journey.

After this, the way to the Pole was clear and, in 1910, Scott set out on his second expedition with the object of attaining it. His ship was the *Terra Nova* and for land transport he relied mainly on Siberian ponies although he also took some dogs and three motor-sledges. A new winter station was set up at Cape Evans on Ross Island and an extensive programme of exploration and research put into operation. One of the scientific expeditions was the

Moon halo and Mount Erebus, watercolour by G. E. Marston, artist on Shackleton's expedition of 1907–9. (Courtesy of the Scott Polar Research Institute)

'worst journey in the world', of which more later.

On the way south, at Melbourne, Australia, Scott had received a telegram from Amundsen, who had led the world to believe he was going to the Arctic, which read: 'Beg leave inform you proceeding Antarctic. Amundsen.' Scott made no public comment and seems to have thought that Amundsen would make an attempt on the Pole from the Weddell Sea side. Then, on a cruise east along the edge of the ice shelf the *Terra Nova* came across the Norwegian ship, *Fram*, and a workman-like base established on the ice at an accessible indentation known as the Bay of Whales. Shackleton had rejected the idea of establishing a base there for fear that the edge of the ice shelf might break off and go out as an iceberg, but Amundsen took the risk and thereby gained a start of 100 kilometres (60 miles) towards the Pole.

Scott refused to be panicked into making a race of it. Using ponies, dogs, motor-sledges and supporting parties to help him establish depots, he set off across the ice shelf at the beginning of November 1911. From the foot of the Beardmore Glacier it was man-hauling for the rest of the way, and at the top of the glacier the last supporting party turned back. From there it was 272 kilometres (169 miles), with a gale in their faces and 54° of frost, across the Polar Plateau, featureless except for 'sastrugi', ridges cut by the wind in the

Captain Oates with some of the ponies on the *Terra Nova*, British Antarctic Expedition 1910–13; photo Herbert Ponting. (Courtesy of the Scott Polar Research Institute)

snow surface. The only way of telling when they had reached the Pole would be from sightings of the sun and calculations of angles and elevations. The only way, that is, if someone else had not already marked the spot with a black flag. Amundsen, in a meticulously planned and professionally-executed journey by dog sledge and ski, had come on a nearly parallel route up the Axel Heiberg Glacier and arrived at the Pole one month and two days earlier on 14 December 1911.[36] The story of how Scott and his four companions, dispirited, short of food and contending with awful weather, perished on the way back has been told too often to need repeating here.[37]

Much has been written about Scott[38] and, after more than half a century during which he was looked on as the quintessential English hero, it was inevitable that some would itch to besmirch the image.[39] Reading the many accounts by his companions on his expeditions – sailor and scientist, British and Norwegian – one is left with a clear impression of a lively and capable mind backed by great integrity, courage and determination. There would have had to have been a most improbable conspiracy in the writing both of

Man-hauling, British Antarctic Expedition 1910–13; photo Herbert Ponting. (Courtesy of the Scott Polar Research Institute)

Storm sun, Antarctica (water-colour)

private diaries and published books had it been otherwise. True, under his command a sharp distinction was drawn between ward-room and lower deck, both in the squalid hovel in which the northern party had to spend a winter [40] and in the civilized milieu of the hut at Cape Evans. This makes us feel uncomfortable now but it was normal for the times and accepted cheerfully and without serious question. With hindsight we can see that Scott made misjudgements which together led to disaster. He allowed, surely unconsciously, the prejudice of his patron, Sir Clements Markham, in favour of man-hauling and against dog-sledges and skis, to blind him to the superiority of the latter form of travel, and he dissipated resources on Siberian ponies and motor-sledges when neither was really proven under polar conditions. He made a last-minute change of plans, including a fifth man in the party and thus slowing down by perhaps a crucial margin the dash for the Pole and the return. These things tipped the balance which the unseasonably bad weather had made precarious. Compared with Amundsen's single-minded professionalism, Scott's efforts at polar travel do look somewhat amateurish.

Taking a sun sight at the South Pole, Norwegian Antarctic Expedition, 14 December 1911. (Amundsen, *The South Pole*, 1912, vol. 2, p.112)

The other side of the coin is that Scott, although he had received no formal training in science, was a scientist of considerable ability at heart and, thanks to his enthusiasm and planning, there was a massive yield of knowledge from his two expeditions, whereas there was none from Amundsen's.

After Scott and Amundsen, Antarctic explorers looked for fresh fields to conquer. The Australian geologist Douglas Mawson, who had been with Shackleton on his *Nimrod* expedition, led his own in the *Aurora* in 1911–14 to an area just west of the Ross Sea. This turned out to be one of the most relentlessly windy places on earth. The story of how, after his two companions on a sledge journey had perished and most of his provisions been lost, he struggled back the 160 kilometres (100 miles) to base, is one of the great epics of survival.

Another epic of survival, not of an individual but of a whole ship's company, was on the 1914–16 British Imperial Trans-Antarctic Expedition, led by Shackleton. The idea had been that the traverse party should land on the Atlantic side of the continent and cross it via the Pole to the Ross Sea. On the second half they were to use depots of supplies laid by another party operating from the Ross Sea side. However, the *Endurance*, carrying Shackleton and the traverse party, was beset and finally crushed and sank in the ice of the Weddell Sea. After drifting for months on the ice, the men managed to get on to Elephant Island in the South Shetlands, whence Shackleton sailed with five companions in the 6-metre (20-foot) *James Caird* across 1300 kilometres (800 miles) of the most turbulent sea in the world to South Georgia. Here he had to cross an uncharted mountain range to reach the whaling

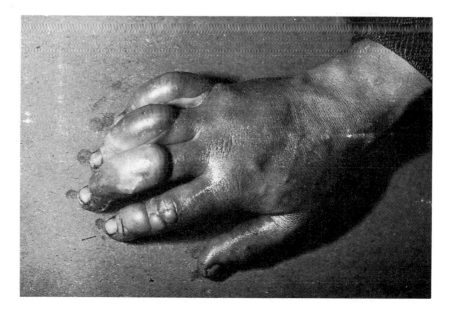

Dr Atkinson's frost-bitten hand, British Antarctic Expedition 1910–13; photo Herbert Ponting. (Courtesy of the Scott Polar Research Institute)

Scott Peak, Lemaire Channel (water-colour)

station at Stromness and, eventually, to arrange rescue for those left behind on Elephant Island. Not a man was lost.[41]

The *Endurance* had been about to sail south when the First World War broke out. Shackleton had immediately offered ship, stores and men to the Admiralty but received a reply from the First Lord, Winston Churchill, thanking him but saying that the expedition should go forward. When they returned to the world in 1917 Shackleton and his men found it vastly changed. Among its other effects, modern war has accelerated technological development, and things such as radio communication, motorized transport and aircraft which became generally available were greatly to enlarge the scope of Antarctic exploration – but not immediately.

The grave of Scott, Wilson and Bowers, 12 November 1912. (Courtesy of the Scott Polar Research Institute)

The major expedition in the post-war decade, the *Discovery Investigations* (1925–39), named after Scott's old ship which was one of the two research vessels used, was concerned with the whaling industry and its work was mainly oceanographic rather than geographic exploration.[42] However, it did, for example, make the first thorough investigation of the South Sandwich Islands. It used radio, of course, but did not need motorized land transport or aircraft. A series of summer exploring expeditions sponsored by the Norwegian whaling magnate Lars Christensen between 1926 and 1937 did use small aircraft later on for reconnaisance and survey. Nevertheless, the first aeroplane flight in the Antarctic was made by the Australian, Sir Hubert Wilkins, in a Lockheed Vega monoplane in November 1928. He made a ten-hour flight from Deception Island down the Peninsula to about 71°20'S. He concluded, erroneously as it turned out, that it was not a peninsula but an archipelago, but the dramatic demonstration that aircraft could be used under Antarctic conditions was the important thing.

An expedition led by Commander Richard Evelyn Byrd, the first major expedition to depart for the Antarctic from the United States for ninety years, really began the extensive application of modern technology to Antarctic exploration. It started simply as a bid for the distinction of flying over the South Pole for the first time. Byrd had flown over the North Pole in 1926, being the first to do so, and at a celebratory dinner he was asked by Amundsen: 'What shall it be now?' Whether his reply, 'The South Pole', was

Leaning on the wind, Adélie Land, Australasian Antarctic Expedition 1911–14; photo Frank Hurley. (Courtesy of the Scott Polar Research Institute)

intended seriously at the time is uncertain but Amundsen, assuming that it was, gave him advice and it soon became a definite intent. This was when the great crash on Wall Street was looming and money was hard to come by, but J. D. Rockefeller Jr and Edsel Ford contributed and Byrd was able to set out with two ships and three aircraft in the late summer of 1928. He established his base, Little America, a community of forty-two men, at the Bay of Whales not far from Amundsen's Framheim.

At this time there were thoughts both in London and Australia that the whole of Antarctica ought to be part of the British Empire, and the fact that Byrd had not obtained permission from the British government for his expedition caused some flurry in official circles. This had the beneficial result for Antarctic exploration that a British-Australian-New Zealand Antarctic Research Expedition (BANZARE) was dispatched in October 1929, under Mawson's leadership in the *Discovery*, to plant the flag on the Antarctic continent south from Cape Town.[43] A small plane, a Gipsy Moth, was taken for reconnaisance and a new stretch of coast, Mac.Robertson Land, was discovered. Valuable hydrographic work was done but there was no inland exploration and BANZARE was outshone by the American achievement.

The centrepiece of the American expedition was a successful sixteen-hour flight to the Pole and back made by Byrd in a three-engined Ford monoplane on 28–9 November 1929. The flight went up the Liv Glacier, at the bottom of which they had refuelled. There was difficulty in gaining sufficient altitude to clear the pass at its head but, by jettisoning their emergency rations, they got over with a few metres to spare. 'The Pole lay in the center of a limitless plain,' wrote Byrd afterwards. 'And that, in brief, is all there is to tell about the South Pole. One gets there, and that is about all there is for the telling. It is the effort to get there that counts.'[44] He did not forget, in his moment of triumph, the three-month labour of Amundsen and the sacrifice of their lives by Scott and his companions in achieving the same spot.

Byrd's radio message to Little America saying that the plane was over the South Pole was by chance picked up by a radio operator in New York and the news was immediately broadcast by loudspeaker in Times Square. Radio had, however, played a more important part than making possible a spectacular bit of publicity. Weather reports transmitted from field parties were an invaluable contribution to the success of the flight. These field parties carried out extensive geological surveys and radio was useful to them, not only for the reassurance of being able to keep in touch with base, but in providing time signals which eliminated a possible source of error in fixing positions. Byrd had taken a Ford snow-mobile, which had front wheels replaced by skis and double caterpillar tracks at the rear, but it became irretrievably bogged down in soft snow and dog-sledges remained

61

for the time being the only reliable means of making long surface journeys. The planes played an important part in placing geological parties in the field. They also carried out surveying using aerial cameras, but if photographs taken with these are to be of any use in mapping, there must be ground control – recognizable features the positions of which are accurately known – and this was not always obtained. Byrd returned to a hero's welcome, a special gold medal, and promotion to Rear-Admiral.

America was now back in the Antarctic arena and henceforth led in logistic innovation. On his return to the Antarctic in 1933–5, Byrd took a heavy Cletrac crawler-type tractor, three Citroën tractors and two Ford snow-mobiles. This time, the motorized transport proved its worth and hauled heavy seismic equipment as far as the polar plateau. However, it was found that bigger is not necessarily better when a 30-tonne snow cruiser was taken on his third expedition in 1939. This contained living quarters and a machine shop as well as carrying fuel and food supplies for a year and a small plane on its roof. It had performed well on sand dunes at home, but, being underpowered and between three and five times too heavy for its tyres to support on snow, it suffered much the same fate as mammoths did in Siberia, and got bogged down.

The first flight from one side of the Antarctic continent to the other was made by another American, Lincoln Ellsworth, in November 1935. With Herbert Hollick-Kenyon as his pilot, he took off from Dundee Island, at the tip of the Peninsula, in a single-engined Northrup monoplane across 3200 kilometres (2000 miles) of unknown territory and through unpredictable weather. Even by Antarctic standards this was an act of supreme courage; the excruciating drudgery of man-hauling a sledge, when at least one has one's feet on the ground and there is the possibility of extricating oneself from danger by one's own physical effort, might to most of us seem preferable to trusting to a fallible machine to preserve one from certain death.

Ellsworth was a rather shy, quiet and seemingly frail man who carried with him as a talisman an ammunition belt which once belonged to his hero, Wyatt Earp, the Texan border marshal. The two-way radio which they took failed because a terminal in the transmitter burnt out, and the last message from them was received after they had been in the air for eight hours. With four landings *en route* they arrived safely, but a little short of their objective, the Bay of Whales, because of lack of fuel. They were thought to be lost, but the British research vessel *Discovery II* sent to search for them found them ensconced in Little America and three days later their own ship, the *Wyatt Earp*, arrived.[45]

They had discovered the Eternity Range, with the three peaks which Ellsworth named Mounts Faith, Hope and Charity, the Sentinel Range, and Ellsworth Land, named after his father, but perhaps more importantly they had completed the establishment of the aeroplane as a practical means of transport in the Antarctic. Planes are not only comparatively safer and incomparably quicker than other ways of getting about but extend the range of observation enormously – at 2 metres (6 feet) above ground level an observer sees the horizon at 2.8 nautical miles, whereas at 3050 metres (10,000 feet) it is at 114.6 nautical miles. An autogyro taken by the second Byrd expedition was the first vertical take-off machine to operate in the Antarctic and this, too, has since proved its worth.

What still remains the most massive single deployment of men and resources ever made in the Antarctic was Operation Highjump, dispatched in 1946–7 by the United States to reassert its interest in this region.[46] It involved 4700 men, thirteen ships and nine aircraft. The fleet included two ice-breakers, *Northwind* and *Burton Island*, the first to operate in the Antarctic. These proved invaluable but the submarine *Sennet* did not, becoming a great liability at the surface among pack ice. Combination wheel and ski landing gear, jet-assisted take-off and helicopters were introduced, but the latter were not used at the time to help in getting parties into the field although they demonstrated their value for this later on. Twice daily synoptic weather charts for the whole Antarctic, airborne magnetometers to assist in geological exploration, and improved methods of aerial photography were among the other innovations.

While the logistics of Antarctic exploration continued to develop, the politics of the Antarctic became more involved and fissile. No government was very sure what use this continent might be; some were content to leave it as it was, but others felt that claims must be asserted if only to prevent rivals from establishing themselves. In this uneasy situation scientists, intent on their own business, decided on another polar year, like that which had been held in 1882–3. This developed into the International Geophysical Year of 1957 which directed special attention to the Antarctic and most happily and unintentionally provided a way out for the politicians. Chapter Ten will say more about this; for the moment all that needs to be noted is that the International Geophysical Year was a resounding success and led to the establishment of permanent bases in Antarctica by eleven nations. These nations, and others which have joined them, have worked with real co-operation and harmony ever since. Antarctica has been criss-crossed by aerial surveys and surface traverses so that, although much remains unvisited, the general features of the continent have been established. The sciences of the Antarctic – oceanography, glaciology, geology, geophysics, meteorology, ionospherics and biology – have expanded enormously.

Antarctica is often described as 'a continent for science' but while coastlines and mountain ranges have been mapped and volume on volume of scientific information has accumulated, human perception of the Antarctic scene has been deepening too. It is the race for the Pole and the spectacular tragedy of Scott's return from losing it that have most caught the public imagination, at least in the English-speaking world. Largely for this reason it is Scott's last expedition that has played the major part in shaping the general view of Antarctica. There have been far more books, films and television programmes about it than about any other expedition. There is even a major symphony; Vaughan Williams, having written the music for the Ealing Studios film *Scott of the Antarctic*, was gripped by the subject and reshaped his music into the *Sinfonia Antartica*, first performed in 1953. It makes imaginative use of tone colour to convey the Antarctic scene – which Vaughan Williams had not seen, of course – with an awesome incursion of the organ to represent the ice-falls of the Transantarctic Mountains. There is a heroic main theme with overtones of tragic failure. In the last movement the sound of a wind-machine and, surprisingly but very effectively, wordless singing by female voices, reassert the loneliness and indifference to human affairs of the Antarctic.

Besides scientific talent, there was great ability in painting, writing and photography among Scott's men and in the hut at Cape Evans there was a cheerful and relaxed atmosphere in which it could be exercised. On one level it found expression in the *South Polar Times*, a light-hearted miscellany of mainly satirical articles, verse and sketches, printed and bound on the spot. The flavour may be given a few lines of photographer Ponting's verses on *The Sleeping Bag*:

> As the furside is the outside, and the skinside is the inside,
> One side likes the skinside inside, and the furside on the outside.
> Others like the skinside outside, and the furside on the inside;
> As the skinside is the hard side, and the furside is the soft side.[47]

A poem *The Barrier Berg* by geologist Frank Debenham is more serious:

> Breasting the slow-heaving, limitless swell,
>   Child of the snow and the far-reaching tides,
> Proudly I swing, sheer-riven, clean-cornered,
>   Dipping awash my immaculate sides.
> Drift of the ocean beneath me, compelling,
>   Drives me athwart half the winds of the world,
> Soft tepid seas, embracing encave me,
>   Foam-lathered billows beset me upcurled.
> Broken and tilted, sun-wasted, sea-drunken,
>   Once more to the shores of the Southland returned,
> Aground on a shoal I await the last mercy,
>   Swift death and complete in the cold sea interned.[48]

That is certainly evocative, but an oceanographer might quibble about the third line from the end.

Herbert Ponting was a photographer of genius, self-styled as a 'camera artist', who had already established himself by twenty years of travel and photography before going south with Scott. Although his equipment looks primitive now, he produced photographs of landscape, interiors and men that can scarcely be surpassed today. He had an eye for the picturesque and was not above fixing things to ensure that they were. He smashed all negatives with which he was not completely satisfied. His film of the expedition is not so spectacular as his still photographs and perhaps for that reason is more true to the Antarctic scene. Without doubt it deserves a place in the history of the documentary cinema. He experimented with the colour process known as Autochrome which had been developed a few years earlier by the Lumière brothers. Ponting considered that the plates had deteriorated by the time he came to use them and his best efforts, although acceptable, are dull in comparison with the brilliance of present-day colour photography.

Herbert Ponting and his telephoto camera, British Antarctic Expedition 1910–13. (Courtesy of the Scott Polar Research Institute)

Herbert Ponting at work in his dark room, British Antarctic Expedition 1910–13. (Courtesy of the Scott Polar Research Institute)

Another photographer of a calibre almost equal to that of Ponting was Frank Hurley,[49] who took part in the expeditions of Mawson and of Shackleton in the *Endurance*. When the *Endurance* was crushed he was ordered to leave his plates and films behind, a saving of weight in the journey that was to come being vital. Against orders and at great risk he rescued them from the sinking vessel, and Shackleton relented to the extent of letting him keep some films and plates, the remaining ones being destroyed to prevent any second thoughts. So there survived the magnificent pictures of *Endurance* beset in the Antarctic night, the epic cine-film *In the Grip of the Polar Ice*, and the poignant snap-shots of survival and rescue on Elephant Island.

Edward Wilson, chief scientist on Scott's last expedition, was an outstanding person. A deeply religious man, he was liked and respected by his fellows, to whom he was known as Uncle Bill, and was the king-pin which held the expedition together. He was a great admirer of Turner and a gifted and prolific artist himself. His chief concern as a professional zoologist was to record Antarctic animals in meticulous detail but he also painted the Antarctic scene – ice, mountains and sky– with both scientific accuracy and artistic integrity. Here is Cherry-Garrard's description of his methods:

> The afternoon was like the morning, save that the sun was now sinking behind the Western Mountains. These autumn effects were among the most beautiful sights of the world, and it was now that Wilson made the sketches for many of the water-colours which he afterwards painted at

Winter Quarters. The majority were taken from the summit of Observation Hill, crouching under the lee of the rocks into which, nearly two years after, we built the Cross which now stands to commemorate his death and that of his companions. He sketched quickly with bare fingers and mittened hands, jotting down the outlines of hills and clouds, and pencilling in the colours by name. After a minute, more or less, the fingers became too cold for such work, and they must be put back into the wool and fur mitts until they are again warm enough to continue. Pencil and sketch book, a Winsor and Newton, were carried in a little blubber-stained wallet on his belt.[37]

His finished paintings were worked up in a crowded ward-room by the light of an acetylene lamp. Under such conditions the accuracy of his colour values is little short of miraculous. His paintings, being mostly held by scientific institutions and reproduced in specialist books, are not as widely appreciated as they should be.[50] David Smith has made the comment that

E. A. Wilson working up a watercolour painting, British Antarctic Expedition 1910–13; photo Herbert Ponting. (Courtesy of the Scott Polar Research Institute)

British landscape painters, unlike their French counterparts, cannot count on the weather and so, being accustomed to work quickly to catch the transient movement of cloud and light, rain and storm, are more suited by training to work in the Antarctic. In this sense Edward Wilson is a supreme example of his school.

Scott, in his last entries in his diary, had a directness and urgency that still have the power to move us. His assistant zoologist, Apsley Cherry-Garrard, was greatly affected by the Scott tragedy and expressed this in writing the book which undoubtedly has the greatest literary merit of any in Antarctic literature. Its title, *The Worst Journey in the World*,[37] refers to an excursion in the company of Wilson and Bowers in the depth of winter to collect eggs of the emperor penguin, but the book gives the story of the whole expedition and he wrote as well on the satisfactions of Antarctica as on its horrors. Probably more people have got their idea of the Antarctic from this book than from any other source. George Bernard Shaw, who was a friend of Cherry-Garrard's, wrote of it as follows:

> The winter journey ventured upon by three members of the Scott Antarctic Expedition solely to obtain a scrap of evidence in evolutionary natural history was a very horrible experience. Compared with it Amundsen's victorious rush to the South Pole seems as cheerful as a trip to Margate. Even Dante's exploration of the icebound seventh circle of hell shews that men cannot imagine the worst that they can suffer. It was perhaps the only real stroke of luck in Scott's ill-fated expedition that Cherry-Garrard, the one survivor of the winter journey, happened to be able to describe it so effectively that the reader forgets how comfortable he is in his armchair, and remembers the tale with a shiver as if he had been through it himself. It is told without the slightest literary affectation or artificiality, and is thus – what few travellers' tales are – absolutely and convincingly credible.[51]

There are now over forty bases, the largest, the US McMurdo base on Ross Island, being virtually a small town, and the population of the continent is as much as 800 in winter, rising to over 2000 in summer. Antarctic travel, by plane, ice-breaker or ice-strengthened vessel, Sno-cat or even skidoo, is rapid and comparatively comfortable, although still not entirely safe. Given influence in the right quarters and good planning it would be possible to get from London to the Pole itself within forty-eight hours. Communication by radio is immediate. Air photography, radio echo-sounding and satellite surveillance give overall views. Colour photography of a technical excellence undreamed of by Ponting and Hurley and sound recording of a perfection unimagined by Drygalski give faithful records of detail. Indeed, colour photography flourishes remarkably in Antarctica. Nearly everyone who goes

The *Endurance* beset, Weddell Sea, midwinter 1915; photo Frank Hurley. (Courtesy of the Scott Polar Research Institute)

68

there takes a 35 mm single lens reflex camera with stacks of colour film, and rivalry and emulation ensure an extremely high standard of photography among these amateurs. There are also professional photographers of great distinction, such as Eliot Porter and Eric Hosking, who have worked recently in the far south.[52] As a result, nearly every publication and illustrated lecture on Antarctic matters has wonderful pictures.

With all this comes a nagging disquiet. Our technological ability to insulate ourselves from a harsh environment and to record sights and sounds for experiencing at second-hand is cutting us off from direct apprehension of the Antarctic world. It is all too easy to take a colour photograph without really looking at the subject and, when taken, it may attract no more than a superficial glance. Such separation from the thing itself is seen most acutely at the base at McMurdo. Here the Americans have established a centre of efficient logistics and high technology which enables scientists to carry out their investigations with maximum dispatch and a minimum of unproduc-

The *Endurance* crushed, Weddell Sea, November 1915; photo Frank Hurley. (Courtesy of the Scott Polar Research Institute)

Sun, storm clouds and icebergs (water-colour)

tive time. Time, that is, which administrators would describe as unproductive but which might possibly be used in contemplation and creative thought about the Antarctic scene. The scientists get out into the field, but as soon as possible they and their data are taken back to civilization, leaving lesser mortals to look after the stations. The base personnel who provide the back-up for the scientists are insulated by extra comforts and artificial distractions against the unfriendly environment. It seems that few go outside the confines of the base and few wish to remain longer than they have to.

British Antarctic research is in a somewhat better state. Since its chosen territory is less suitable for flying, sea voyages through the labyrinths of the Antarctic Peninsula enforce more perception of weather and scenery, and traditionally the distinction between base and field personnel is blurred. The 'jolly', in which diesel mechanic and cook go off on a recreational trip with scientist and field assistant to scale a mountain, cross a glacier or visit an island, does occasionally result in disaster – always because of forgetfulness of safety regulations – but otherwise does tremendous things for morale and appreciation of the environment. In the British Antarctic Survey those who do not overwinter feel themselves of inferior race. But, British or American, whatever the national organization, increasing efficiency of logistics and extending bureaucratic control seem bound to cut down the time which scientists and others can have to take in the non-material qualities of the Antarctic.

A brave and thought-provoking attempt has been made by Stephen J. Pyne in his book *The Ice* to bring the two cultures together and to interpret for the humanities the meaning of our scientific knowledge of the Antarctic.[53] His lyrical account of ice as the determinant of this most alien landscape on our planet leads him to the conclusion that Antarctica is a simultaneous emblem of our modern age of isolation and of the strength of the natural world. He sees the outstanding trait of the ice as its preternatural emptiness; 'its greatest asset is not any resource it possesses but the stripped and reradiated revelations it makes about those who stare into it'.

Perhaps, staring into the ultimate emptiness of the level ice of the polar plateau in the diffuse light of a white-out, ordinary mortals can do little more than echo Captain Scott's 'Great God, this is an awful place', but around the edge of the continent, where there is interplay between rocks, sea and ice, there is more scope for the artist. Here, by looking and making us see what he sees, he can provide some antidote to the loss of direct contact with the actuality of Antarctica. The primary function of the artist on the earlier expeditions was to make topographical records, but, as the selection included in this book shows, some of these managed to capture something of the awesomeness of the Antarctic as well. As photography developed, this function of the artist became less necessary but nevertheless amateurs

The *Discovery* in winter quarters, 1903. Watercolour by E. A. Wilson. (Courtesy of the Scott Polar Research Institute)

Evening rays, Atlantic (water-colour)

persisted and many, from Joseph Hooker and Edward Wilson onwards, who have worked as scientists in the Antarctic have sought to record their impressions in sketches and paintings, with variable results. Alister Hardy, chief zoologist in the *Discovery* investigations around South Georgia in the 1920s, illustrated his book *Great Waters* with his own water-colour sketches of Antarctic seascapes and animals.[54] A colleague of his, Rolfe Gunther, was also a fine artist in line and water-colour, recording the South Georgian peaks and elephant seals yawning 'among the tussock grass with the terrible boredom of club-men'[55]. Gunther, alas, died young in the Second World War when he was accidentally shot by a sentry when returning to barracks one dark night. A more recent example of the amateur artist in Antarctica is Dr R. M. Laws, Director of the British Antarctic Survey from 1973 to 1987, who has also been a prolific producer of fine water-colours of Antarctic scenes. Thus some scientists evidently think that science does not say everything about Antarctica and several official agencies have been enlightened enough to send professional painters south.

Among these have been Edward Seago, who accompanied HRH Prince Philip on a cruise down the Antarctic Peninsula in RRS (Royal Research Ship) *John Biscoe* in 1957. Sidney Nolan did twenty-six paintings after a short trip south as a guest of the United States Navy in 1963–4. His landscapes are readily assimilated but others of his paintings are more recondite; the art critic Elwyn Lynn reviewing an exhibition for *The Australian* wrote as follows:

> Never has man looked so isolated and vulnerable as the men in the South's vast desolation. They are dressed in dreary grey; their sunglasses turn their anguished gaze inwards; one is hollow-eyed, desperate and not unlike Nolan himself.
>
> Some look indigenous, yet unwanted; some are wafted up like mirages, real and unreal. One, on a brown pony, is naked, his leg a brilliant green . . . The masts of a ship, caught in the cold, blue ice, break into yellow foliage in protest against the barrenness. In another, a bird swoops towards a crag of ice while the indigo sea beyond plunges to eternity. Two figures, almost indiscernible, stand beneath a reddened flag streaming in the wind. All the while the landscape heaves, glaciers writhe and undulate, almost cascade with slashed and curdled paint.[56]

Water-colour by E. A. Wilson of the slopes of Mount Erebus and the ramp from Cape Evans during Scott's second Antarctic expedition, 1910–13. (Courtesy of the Scott Polar Research Institute)

'Nolan's Antarctica', says the critic, 'is the Anxious and Apprehensive Land' – not a view that would be shared, perhaps, by one returning to the rat-race of a big city after a spell down south. The paintings of Maurice Conly, who has twice visited Antarctica as official artist to the New Zealand Antarctic Division, are more representational. They depict life on base as well as landscape and a selection has been published in his book *Ice on my Pallete*.[57] Incidentally, the water-colour artist Austen Deans has made a virtue of the paint freezing on the paper but, on the whole, this is something to be avoided.

David Smith, whose paintings provided the stimulus to write this book, went south with the British Antarctic Survey in the Austral summers of 1975–6 and 1979–80. He has written of his work as follows:

> It was a challenge for artistic effort, with which few artists have had the privilege to be faced. Fortunately, all art materials needed could go on the ship with me. There was no need to be selective over bulky painting gear – canvasses, drawing boards, and easels – as when undertaking a motoring painting tour.
>
> During the first voyage I worked mainly in oils. On the second voyage . . . I worked primarily in the water-colour medium. My aim was to record the entire voyage in water-colour drawings. By adopting a strict, disciplined daily routine I began my studies of the sea, coastlines, ports, icescapes and the British bases. I took good care to annotate the pictures with the exact time of execution, latitude and longitude and, of course, name of the area or place. I returned with a collection of more than five hundred works . . .
>
> My work was greatly aided by being allowed to paint from the port and starboard wings of the bridge of the ship. From these vantage points, with the ship travelling at a moderate–average speed of eight knots, the coastline does not appear to pass by too rapidly. It is therefore possible to work at a steady, comfortable pace, recording the varying scenes with a good deal of topographical accuracy. Another piece of good luck was being allowed to work from the enclosed conning tower, high up on the ship's mainmast. From this lofty vantage point there was a 'grandstand' view of Antarctica. In all directions, as the ship forced her way through the pack ice, there were endless exciting vistas of geometric patterns made by the ice floes. I vividly recall one magical evening during the 1975–6 voyage when we left the Brunt Ice Shelf at Halley very late in the season, because the relief to the base had been held up by a six-day blizzard. The sun was very low and, from the conning tower, the pack ice to the horizon all round was drenched in tints of pink, cerulean blue, viridian green and violet . . .
>
> Many people would presume that in Antarctica the painter would be faced with a perpetual vista of whiteness. The reverse is the truth. The refraction of light, from the multitude of differently angled ice planes, presents to the eye endless tints of subtle colour which would have entranced the great Impressionist painters such as Monet, Renoir, Pissarro and Sisley. Nevertheless, this gentler side of the Antarctic scene can suddenly and dramatically change. The wind and driving snow present more

Sketch by E. A. Wilson of three men in a pyramid tent, Scott's second expedition 1910–13. (Courtesy of the Scott Polar Research Institute)

Sledging in April.
Camping after dark.

violent themes for the Expressionist painter. Turner, Nolde, Vlaminck and Ryder would have revelled in the flying spume from the waves in the force ten gales and the slabs of two-metres-thick pack ice, tossed about as if they were playing cards.

The technical aspect of painting out of doors at the bases, and in the ice-covered landscape, presented no difficulties. I was equipped with a strong easel, the legs of which wedged firmly into the ice. Oil paint became very stiff in the intense cold and I found it much more manageable to push it around on the canvas with the palette knife. Anti-freeze, in the form of duty free gin, laced the water and eased the flow of the watercolour paints. During the bad weather, shelter in a hut, or in the chimney-like entrances to the submerged Halley base, enabled me to get something down on paper or canvas, no matter what the climatic conditions.

To get even the briefest note, or sketch, recorded at the time of experiencing the scene, is of vital necessity. The mind thinks three-dimensionally around the form of the subject observed and the hand describes it on the paper or canvas. For the artist, photographs, in relation to his work, can only be useful for reference. From these on-the-spot sketches the spirit of the moment can be captured in the subsequent studio developments. On brilliantly sunny days reflection of the light from the ice surface can be hazardous for the eyes and sunglasses should be worn. Fortunately, my eyes are deeply set and the glare was not harmful or troublesome over short periods. Obviously the wearing of sunglasses would change the tonality and colour range of the subject.

Many days are spent at sea away from land. During these periods I made a series of over two hundred pencil or chalk drawings of the great variety of characters on board. There were also numerous studies made of the many activities of running the ship: deck maintenance, navigation, engineering and catering.[58]

His pictures in this book, which are all from the South Atlantic sector of Antarctica in which the British Antarctic Survey operates, illustrate his conclusion that 'for the artist, Antarctica provides an endless, inexhaustible panorama of pictorial images'.

Chapter Three

Gateways to Antarctica

THERE ARE two main gateways into Antarctica, both where southernmost outposts of civilization extend towards weak points in the continent's natural defences, and these, other things being equal, have been used by most expeditions. One leads from ports in Australia or New Zealand to the Ross Sea, the other from ports around the southern tip of South America to the Antarctic Peninsula. Only the USSR among the major Antarctic powers does not use these routes regularly; five of her seven stations are off these beaten paths and are serviced directly from the mother country by ice-breaker, then tractor-train and transport aircraft.

The Australian ports of Sydney and Hobart were used by the great expeditions of Balleny, Wilkes, d'Urville and Ross in the mid-nineteenth century which established that there was a continent and showed the way to approach it. All these expeditions were treated with great hospitality and friendship by the Australians. Wilkes sailed into harbour at Sydney under cover of darkness and produced consternation by hoisting the American flag at daybreak. The Governor was grateful – it made a point about the defences of Sydney which he had thus far urged unsuccessfully on a parsimonious Council. Astonishment was expressed that the Americans did not appear to be either Negroes or Red Indians, and on their part the Americans were surprised to find a prosperous and civilized colony instead of the 'den of abominations, tenanted exclusively by English criminals, the offscouring of the earth' that they expected. The Australians compared the condition and equipment of the American ships unfavourably with those of the *Erebus* and *Terror*, and Wilkes had trouble with some of his officers who, apart from various other grievances, were not anxious to leave the comfort of Sydney for the rigours of the Antarctic. However, after a lavish and successful farewell party given by Wilkes, the squadron sailed for the south in reasonably good heart and with the genuine good wishes of their hosts.[21]

The *Astrolabe* and *Zelée* put in at Hobart both before and after their venture to the south. Their crews were in poor health; after being a guest of the garrison, d'Urville, whose digestion was weak at the best of times, wrote: '*Malheureusement nos estomacs délabrés ne pouvaient encore nous permettre de jouir entièrement de l'amiable invitation de MM. les officiers anglais.*' ('Unfortunately our disordered stomachs did not as yet permit us to enjoy to the full the kind invitation of the English officers.')[19] Recuperated, they were able properly to enjoy a ball given for them by Lady Franklin, the Governor's wife, before they sailed south. On his return, d'Urville authorized the publication in the local newspapers of an account of his discovery of Adélie Land.

When Ross arrived in Hobart five months after d'Urville had departed for home, he had not only this news of the French discovery but also of that of Wilkes, who, ignoring his instructions from the US government to keep his explorations secret, sent Ross a friendly letter from New Zealand enclosing a chart of his cruise along the coast of what is now Wilkes Land. Ross does not appear to have been much put out that he had been forstalled by both the French and the Americans in the area which he had been instructed to explore, nor was he adverse to departing from those instructions.[59] Following up Balleny's finding of open sea at latitude 69°S to the east of the region explored by d'Urville and Wilkes and confident of the superiority of his ships, he took the course which, as we have seen, brought spectacular discoveries.

Ross's ships were jubilantly welcomed back in Hobart. The mate of the *Erebus*, in a letter home, recorded that about twenty-five of the crew 'had comfortable lodgings in jail having nearly taken the Town owing to the Hospitality of the Inhabitants'. The Royal Victoria Theatre put on a specially written play, *Antarctic Expedition*, of which Act II presented 'a splendid view of the Volcanic Mountain' and Act III, 'a grand allegorical tableau, of Science crowning the distinguished navigators Captain Ross and Crozier at the command of Britannia'. The epilogue, at least, seems to have been greeted with acclamation.

> Victory is yours – but in a glorious cause –
> With Science – genius – you have waged your wars
> From pole to pole you've conquered as you run;

> And well you've won, the ocean's icy throne.
> Tasmania hails you as her favoured guest
> And Fame your Triumphs loudly will attest.[59]

Among Australian scientists, Sir Douglas Mawson – who, besides serving with Shackleton, led two major expeditions of his own – was particularly active in the Antarctic. For a long time Australian attention was restricted to two peri-Antarctic islands, Macquarie and Heard. Two world wars and a world depression delayed the realization of Mawson's vision of a permanent Australian presence on the continent itself until 1954 when a station named after him was set up in Mac. Robertson Land.[60] He died in 1958 and is commemorated by the Mawson Institute for Antarctic Research in the University of Adelaide. During the International Geophysical Year, the various Australian projects became officially grouped as ANARE (Australian National Antarctic Research Expeditions), with headquarters in Melbourne. This is administered by the Antarctic Division of the Department of External Affairs and, appropriately, now has its headquarters at Kingston, near Hobart.

The great expeditions of Scott and Shackleton were well supported in Australia but made New Zealand, which offered a port 800 kilometres (500 miles) nearer to Ross Island, their point of departure. Lyttelton, the port for the city of Christchurch on the east coast of the South Island, provided a sheltered harbour with all facilities. It was there that the *Discovery* expedition made its final preparations before going south. There was great kindness and intelligent interest from both public bodies and private individuals; charges for harbour dues, docking and wharfage were waived, the railway gave free travel to members of the expeditions, who were entertained in a most friendly fashion as individuals. Special trains from Christchurch carried thousands to see the *Discovery* sail. Tragically, in the excitement a young seaman, Charles Bonner, fell from the top of the mainmast and was killed. It was found afterwards that he had taken a bottle of whisky up aloft with him. Shackleton's *Nimrod* expedition was greeted as warmly as was the *Discovery* and there were 30,000 people to see it sail. The New Zealand government paid half the cost of towing the ship down to the Antarctic Circle so that coal might be saved for the heavy work in the ice. Scott's last expedition dealt with the same problem by taking on more coal at Port Chalmers, 300 kilometres (200 miles) to the south, after sailing from Lyttelton. Edward Wilson described the send-off from Lyttelton in his diary as:

> Very pretty and very exciting, for the harbour was crowded with people and every ship in the place was decked with flags, and sirens and hooters and gunfiring to say nothing of a number of tugs and small craft literally loaded up with friends and sightseers from Christchurch and Lyttelton, all

to accompany the *Terra Nova* out of the harbour and out to the Heads.[61]

Wilson travelled by train with his wife to Dunedin and on to Port Chalmers and there said what was to be his final goodbye to her:

> Dunedin had been given a special holiday to see us off at 2.30 pm. We were boisterously and very cheerily seen off and Ory was with us on board to the last when she had to go off on to a tug – and there on the bridge I saw her disappear out of sight waving happily, a goodbye that will be with one till the day I see her again in this world or the next – I think it will be in this world and some time in 1912.[62]

It was at Oamaru, a small port between Christchurch and Dunedin, that two years later the *Terra Nova* put in quietly to dispatch the tragic news of the South Pole party before returning to Lyttelton harbour with her flags at half-mast.

Lyttelton today still feels at the edge of beyond – a small but active port surrounded by the low grass and scrub-covered hills which were once the walls of a volcanic crater. The tug which handled the polar ships is still there and Quail Island, where Scott and Shackleton quarantined their dogs and ponies, still remains undeveloped. Christchurch retains some evidence of its connection with the heroic age of Antarctic exploration – Kathleen Scott's white marble version of the statue of her husband stands by the River Avon and the Canterbury Museum has one of the finest Antarctic collections there is – but it is now a large city which has become the busy forward base for the most massive of present-day Antarctic programmes as well as being the headquarters of the New Zealand Antarctic Division.

In 1928 Byrd made Dunedin his port of departure on his way to set up an unauthorized base in a sector of the Antarctic claimed by the British Crown on behalf of New Zealand. He and his men nonetheless met with unstinted kindness and co-operation. As he himself wrote: 'Had we been Englishmen, on an English errand, we could not have been better treated.'[44] He returned there on his second expedition. When it came to the International Geophysical Year (IGY), American effort was again concentrated in the Ross Sea area and, after a hard-ice runway had been established on McMurdo Sound by the naval Operation Deep Freeze I, depended heavily on air transport. Since 1957, when its newspapers gave the IGY coverage appropriate to it as a major world event, Christchurch has been the main United States staging-post from which the giant C-130 Hercules four-engined turboprop planes depart for Williams Field, McMurdo. In return for providing facilities at Christchurch International Airport for the US Naval Support Force, Antarctica, ITT Antarctic Services Inc. of New Jersey and the United States Antarctic Research Programme, New Zealand gets help with transport both to and from and within Antarctica – a fair exchange provided that weather and their own commitments allow the Americans to fulfil their part of the bargain. Inevitably there is some strain there and some New Zealanders may not be too happy with a wealthy and self-assured partner making free with a region to which New Zealand makes formal claim but, on the whole, the arrangement works well to the benefit of the research programmes of both countries.

Air passage from Christchurch to McMurdo avoids a voyage through tempestuous and iceberg-strewn seas but substitutes its own discomforts and anxieties. A Hercules on Antarctic service lacks even the doubtful amenities offered by commercial airlines on charter and the 3900-kilometre (2400-mile) eight-hour flight is passed sitting cramped in seats of nylon webbing amid a continuous deafening racket. The planes cannot carry enough fuel for the round trip so there comes a point – exactly where depends on weather – when safe return is impossible and they have to go on, regardless of conditions at their destination, without any possibility of diversion to a safer landing ground. Landing at Williams Field can sometimes be terrifying, with turbulence that slams the passengers all over the place, testing seat-belts to their limit and even the strongest stomachs beyond their limits. There may be a white-out that cuts the pilots off from the slightest visual contact with the ground. Even under good conditions a landing on unprepared snow sounds and feels like a crash to the uninitiated. Then the relief of being once more on terra firma is overwhelmed by the shock of Antarctic cold on a body which a few hours before was in the mildness of a New Zealand spring.[63]

So far, these service flights have had a good safety record, although there have been disasters on flights within Antarctica. The most terrible of Antarctic air crashes was that of an Air New Zealand DC10 on Mount Erebus in November 1979 when all 257 people aboard were killed. This put an end to a schedule of regular tourist flights from Australia and New Zealand to the Ross Sea area which had been started in 1977 and enabled some 11,000 aerial sightseers to visit the Antarctic. Scientific stations in Antarctica do not have the resources to look after the safety of such flights nor do they have any legal obligation to provide them with weather forecasts or other assistance.

On the other side of the continent, few of the earlier expeditions used the ports of South America itself as bases. Now, of course, Chilean and Argentinian expeditions use their own ports and airfields for departure to the south. Various tour operators are based in these two countries and provide cruises which visit the South Shetlands and the more northerly parts of the Peninsula. The best of these, on ships such as MV (Motor Vessel) *Linblad Explorer* (now *Society Explorer*) and MV *World Discoverer*, both built especially for Antarctic work, are operated to very high standards of safety. Lectures by

Low sun, ice-floes (oil)

people experienced in Antarctic explorations and science make these cruises highly educational but, on the other hand, because landing places are few, the impact of hundreds of tourists on flora and fauna and any scientific work going on there is considerable. There are also tourist flights from Chilean airfields, mostly going to King George Island in the South Shetlands where the Chilean Teniente Marsh station has a 100-bed hotel for visitors.[64] The first independent commercial airline to be established for Antarctic flights is the Canada-based Antarctic Airways which in 1987–8 operated one DC-4 and two Twin Otter aircraft to fly passengers from Punta Arenas in Chile as far south as the Vinson Massif, the highest mountain in Antarctica, at 78°28'S. The clientele for such a flight obviously comes from the climbing fraternity, but might also come from scientists outside the major national programmes. Such flights are economically possible only because enough fuel can be carried for both the outward and return flights. If fuel has to be air-dropped as far south as the Vinson Massif its cost rises fifty-fold and becomes comparable in value to whisky in British shops.[65]

For many who go south, the Falkland Islands provide the immediate jumping-off point and the first taste of normal human life again on their return. Many famous Antarctic explorers – Palmer, d'Urville, Ross, Shackleton – made the Falklands a departure point for their voyages into Antarctic waters and, for a long time, Stanley, the capital, provided a main depot and communications centre for the British Antarctic Survey. With a larger vessel, RRS *Bransfield*, and satellite communication available, this is no longer necessary nor economic but Stanley still provides a convenient and pleasant rendezvous for the ships and personnel.

Some have found the Falkland Islands grim. HMS *Beagle* with Charles Darwin aboard called there in 1833 and again the following year in a period when British rule had scarcely been established, and Darwin rated the islands lowest in scale among the English colonies he had seen. While he was there a ship-mate was drowned in trying to retrieve from a kelp bed a bird which he had shot, and:

> Mr Smith, who is acting as Governor, came on board, & has related such complicated scenes of cold-blooded murder, robbery, plunder, suffering, such infamous conduct in almost every person who has breathed this atmosphere, as would take two or three sheets to describe.[66]

The countryside seemed to him to have few prospects to redeem this vileness of man and, writing to his sister Catherine, Darwin summed up thus:

> There are fine harbors, plenty of fresh water & good beef: it would doubt-lessly produce the coarser vegetables. In other respects it is a wretched

place: a little time since, I rode across the island & returned in four days: my excursion would have been longer but during the whole time it blew a gale of wind with hail & snow: there is no fire wood bigger than Heath & the whole country is a more or less elastic peat bog. Sleeping out at night was too miserable work to endure it for all the rocks in S. America.[67]

Those who fought in the winter conflict of 1982 would think that this was stating it mildly.

Nevertheless, the Falklands are now visited by tourists and the beautifully illustrated brochures which attract them, although selective in their presentation, are not untruthful. The coastline is spectacular, with rugged cliffs and beaches of white quartzite sand deserted except perhaps for penguins. The weather in summer is usually pleasant with an everchanging pattern of cloud and colour on the mountains. The flora includes many attractive species, some of which are only to be found in the Falklands. One of the most characteristic is diddle-dee, a relative of the British crowberry, found over much of the moorland, and one of the strangest the balsam-bog, in which branches and leaves are compacted to form a hard yellowish-green hemi-spherical mass 60 centimetres (2 feet) or so in diameter. There are vast colonies of sea-birds and seals, some of the birds being surprisingly unafraid

Hunting wild cattle in the Falkland Islands. Woodcut after a sketch by Joseph Hooker. (Ross, *A Voyage of Discovery and Research in the Southern and Antarctic Regions*, 1847, vol. 2, p.240: courtesy of the Scott Polar Research Institute)

Arched iceberg (oil)

of man.[68] Sometimes dolphins can be seen joy-riding in the crests of green translucent waves and, as David Smith noted in his personal diary, groups of gentoo penguins share green marshy fields with cows.

The faunas of the various places mentioned in this chapter include some animals which, although they may not be of the same species, are related to Antarctic types. The Otago Peninsula near Dunedin has albatrosses, yellow-eyed penguins and southern fur seals. Near Hobart can be found the Australian fur seal and the little blue or fairy penguin. Tierra del Fuego and adjacent parts of South America, like the Falklands, have albatrosses, penguins and seals of various kinds. Among these the gentoo penguin and the elephant seal have distributions which extend well into Antarctic waters, so it is worth considering them at a little length here.

The gentoo penguin is a handsome bird, about the same size as the better-known adelie, with a bluish-grey back, white front, orange feet and bill, and a white patch above its eye. They nest in colonies, which may contain a thousand or so birds, preferring a low hill with some greenery on it and moving on to a new site every few years. Strange[68] relates how one group of penguins had evidently shifted their patch across a peninsula until it approached the sea on the other side. Although they then took the shorter route of 2.5 kilometres (1½ miles) on leaving the colony, they nevertheless continued to trudge along the 5 kilometres (3 miles) of the original path

Magellanic or jackass penguins and tussock grass, Falkland Islands. Woodcut after a sketch by Joseph Hooker. Ross, *A Voyage of Discovery and Research in the Southern and Antarctic Regions*, 1847, vol. 2, p.212: courtesy of the Scott Polar Research Institute)

when coming back to it. The gentoo is rather shyer than other Antarctic penguins but, if approached peaceably and greeted with a friendly 'quark!' will engage in conversation for as long as one's patience lasts. It lays two eggs, in a nest of grass, pebbles or twigs, which are incubated for about thirty-three days. The chicks, being clothed fluffily in down, after a time seem to be larger than their parents. When a parent bird returns from the sea with its crop full of krill or squid it is chased by chicks, one of which eventually feeds by inserting its head into the open beak of the regurgitating parent. The chicks are collected in crèches, presumably as a protection against the caracara or johnny rook which preys on them. Further south it is the skua which is the gentoo's chief avian predator. Man is also a predator; these birds used to be rendered down for their oil and Strange has estimated that between 1863 and 1866 over 500,000 gentoo and rockhopper penguins must have been killed in the Falklands to produce the 240,000 litres (63,000 gallons) of oil shipped to Stanley.[68] Their eggs were deemed the most flavoursome by sealers and were still taken under licence in recent times. At sea, it is the sea leopard which is the greatest menace to the gentoo. Having grabbed a penguin in its jaws, this seal shakes it out of its skin before swallowing it. The range of the gentoo extends well down the west side of the Antarctic Peninsula but it is not found in the farthest south.

The elephant seal is so called because the adult male has a short inflatable trunk but the name is also appropriate on account of the size which, again for an adult male, can be as much as 5 metres (16½ feet) in length and 3.6 tonnes in weight. These bulls – moulting in patches, snoring, belching and rumbling, asleep, perhaps immersed to the eyes in a pool of their own ordure – are among the least lovely of God's creatures. They come ashore in spring and are joined a week or two later by the females which are herded into harems, which sometimes may number as many as a hundred, by the more aggressive bulls. The pups are born shortly afterwards and the cows are ready to mate about eighteen days after giving birth. The unsuccessful bulls remain on the fringes and attempt to mate when opportunity offers. If it comes to a fight, the two bulls rear up and lunge at each other, the outcome being a matter of weight. Elephant seals tend to lie together in slovenly heaps and it is just too bad for any unfortunate pup which happens to be in the way. However, it is only if one is met sliding down a gulley between high tussocks that they are a danger to man. They are pathetically easy to kill and their blubber yields an oil as clear and good as that of the whale. Thomas Smith, a mid-nineteenth-century sealer, described his first encounter with them thus:

> After landing, by the command of our mate we advanced with our lances and clubs to the appointed place of slaughter. I walked rather in the rear of the men imagining to myself what shape these creatures could be in, for as

yet, I had not been favored with an opportunity of seeing one of them. I was soon relieved from my anxiety by an immediate attack on the elephants, which to my astonishment and disappointment we found lying down asleep between the bogs. I took my position on one of the bogs to have a good view of them and to keep out of danger, not knowing how they would act on being attacked by the boat's crew who were led on by the mate and boatswain. As soon as the attack was made on them in different positions, they all, being about sixty in number, commenced snorting and some of them roaring, at the same time most of them were endeavouring to make their escape into the water. Poor innocent animals! I could not but pity them, seeing the large tears rolling down from their eyes; they were slaughtered without mercy.[69]

Numbers of elephant seals were greatly reduced in the nineteenth century but never quite to the verge of extinction. Now, they are fully protected. Elephant seals seem to live on squid and fish but little is known of their life at sea, where they are much more graceful and elusive than on land. The total population of between 600,000 and 700,000 animals is distributed among the peri-Antarctic islands, although the occasional one is found as far south as McMurdo Sound.

The vast numbers of sea birds and seals which are found on the coasts of the Falklands suggest to the biologist that the waters surrounding these islands must be highly productive. The inshore waters tell the same tale. There are dense growths of the giant kelp, *Macrocystis pyrifera*, a seaweed up to 60 metres (200 feet) in length, the floating fronds of which form a natural breakwater often extending half a kilometre (quarter of a mile) out to sea. Sometimes the waters are red with swarms of the lobster krill, an engaging miniature lobster-like plankton animal not found in truly Antarctic seas. The Falkland islanders have never been particularly interested in the fishing and nor have fishing concerns in Britain, although the potential value of the fisheries around the islands was drawn to their attention as long ago as 1920. There was interest in the kelp, which yields a valuable chemical, alginic acid, but a pilot plant set up to extract it proved uneconomic. Other nations have been active in exploiting the fish and, following the establishment in 1986 of a 240-kilometre (150-mile) fishing zone around the islands, their dues have transformed the Falklands economy.[70]

Stanley, with a population of under 2000, contains most of the islands' civilian population. It has a toy-town look with neat rows of houses with corrugated iron roofs painted in bright colours – the islands produce nothing suitable for roofing material and corrugated iron is more easily fixed against wind than tiles. The inhabitants show that, given a little shelter, their gardens can do rather better than Darwin predicted and lupins in particular flourish marvellously. Looking across Stanley Harbour one sees the hulks of vessels which, battered by the storms of the Southern Ocean, managed to fight their way to their last resting place here, and on the opposite hillside, picked out in white quartzite stones, the names of famous ships such as *Barracouta*, *Protector* and *Beagle*. One feels at the end of the world.

Due south, about 1500 kilometres (900 miles) away, is the tip of the Antarctic Peninsula. Halley, the British base, is more than twice that distance to the south-south-east across the Weddell Sea and it is nearly 1600 kilometres (1000 miles) just south of east to the island of South Georgia. These distances are formidable but less than that from Christchurch to McMurdo. With the opening of the Mount Pleasant airport, which with its 3-kilometre (2-mile) landing strip is one of the best in the South Atlantic, the Falklands provide an excellent forward base for expeditions to the Antarctic. Indeed, in March 1987 the first US civilian aircraft landed at Mount Pleasant, bringing a hundred scientists and engineers as part of the International Ocean Drilling Programme to carry out geological investigations in the Weddell Sea area. The Falklands could become the major international support base for airborne Antarctic expeditions.[71]

For the present, however, we must set out on the Southern Ocean rather than skip over it.

Port Stanley (water-colour)

Misty day, Lemaire Channel (water-colour)

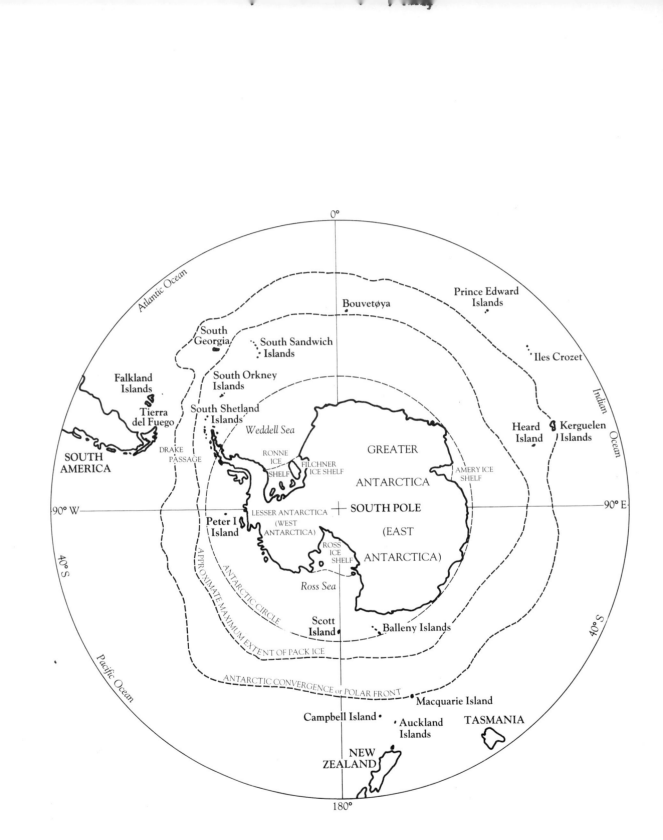

0°

Atlantic Ocean

Prince Edward
Islands

Bouvetøya

South
Georgia

South Sandwich
Islands

Iles Crozet

Falkland
Islands

South Orkney
Islands

Indian Ocean

Tierra
del Fuego

South Shetland
Islands

Weddell Sea

Heard
Island

Kerguelen
Islands

SOUTH
AMERICA

DRAKE
PASSAGE

RONNE
ICE
SHELF

FILCHNER
ICE SHELF

GREATER

ANTARCTICA

AMERY ICE
SHELF

90° W

Peter I
Island

LESSER ANTARCTICA
(WEST
ANTARCTICA)

SOUTH POLE

90° E

(EAST

ANTARCTICA)

ROSS
ICE
SHELF

40° S

ANTARCTIC CIRCLE

APPROXIMATE MAXIMUM EXTENT OF PACK ICE

Ross Sea

Scott
Island

Balleny Islands

40° S

ANTARCTIC CONVERGENCE or POLAR FRONT

Pacific Ocean

Macquarie Island

Campbell Island

Auckland
Islands

TASMANIA

NEW
ZEALAND

180°

Chapter Four

The Southern Ocean

T HE WIDE EXPANSE of sea that surrounds Antarctica extends northwards in the three enormous lobes of the Atlantic, Pacific and
Indian Oceans. There is a world ocean and our subdivisions of it
are arbitrary. The Southern Ocean is defined by the British *Antarctic Pilot*
as: 'the circumpolar body of water lying N of the Antarctic Continent, the N
limits of which are not precisely defined but approximately Latitude 55°S'.
To placate Argentina and Chile, who prefer to emphasize separation rather
than continuity in their back yards, the Intergovernmental Oceanographic
Commission puts it in the plural – Southern Oceans – and US oceanographers are advised not to give it capital letters.[77] Oddly enough, within this
huge indefinite expanse of sea there is a clear line of demarcation put there
by Nature herself. This is the Antarctic Convergence or – although the two
terms are not quite synonymous oceanographically – the Polar Front, and
most scientists prefer to use this as the northern boundary of Antarctic
waters.

Cook and other early explorers noticed that as they sailed south the
Antarctic came upon them abruptly, with clear skies, reasonable temperatures and deserted seas usually changing suddenly to fogs, near freezing
conditions, and an abundance of sea birds. Later it was found that there was
also a change in the surface temperature of the sea; sometimes a vessel lying
across the boundary might register a difference of two or three degrees
between bow and stern, as well as a difference in the plankton. These things
mark the Convergence, a front or discontinuity formed where cold water,
less salty because of melting ice and flowing outwards from around the

The Southern Ocean and
Antarctica

Antarctic Continent, dips beneath the warmer and more salty sub-Antarctic water further north. The Convergence encircles the continent as a remarkably constant line undulating between latitudes 50° and 60°S and the logs of the eighteenth-century voyagers show that it was in the same position in the past. 'Do you think you can draw lines on the living water?' was a question put into the mouth of Eleanor of Aquitaine by Christopher Fry in his play *Curtmantle*, to which an oceanographer might reply that nature does just that on a dramatic scale.

There are other, hidden, demarcations. Outside the continental shelf the Southern Ocean is mostly more than 4000 metres (13,000 feet) deep and much of it goes down to between 5000 and 6000 metres (16,500 and 20,000 feet). If measurements of temperature and salinity are made through the water column down to such depths, it is found that there are three distinct layers in it. On top is cold water of relatively low salt content, evidently produced by dilution of seawater with fresh water from melting ice. This layer is about 200 metres (650 feet) thick. Below it is warm water – when an Antarctic oceanographer talks of warm water he means it is two or three degrees above freezing – which is heavier and stays below because its higher salinity more than compensates for the temperature-related decrease in density. This Antarctic intermediate water extends down to about 1500 metres (5000 feet). Below it is cold, saline, bottom water.

These water masses are not static but circulate in a pattern which results from two main sets of forces, one latitudinal and circumpolar, the other meridional, that is, north-south. The circumpolar circulation depends on the winds. The Antarctic ice cap, which receives only about four-tenths as much solar heat as other parts of the world and reflects most of this back into space, is the Earth's greatest heat sink and as such generates major features of atmospheric circulation. The surface air in contact with it is cold, but above it is a layer of warm air flowing southwards from the temperate regions and this, as it becomes chilled, sinks over the polar region and then returns, spreading northwards from the centre. As these winds flow down the slope of the ice dome they become deflected as a result of the earth's rotation to blow towards the west. Thus, near the continent and out to about 65°S, there is a current in the sea, often called the East Wind Drift, which flows from east to west as far as the configuration of the coastline allows.

Further north there is a wide belt extending between 55–60°S and 40°S which is dominated by the prevailing westerlies which roar unhindered round the globe. These set up the West Wind Drift which extends throughout the depth of the ocean as the Antarctic Circumpolar Current. Only in the Drake Passage, between South America and the Peninsula, and south of Australia is there any restriction on the flow, which amounts to 235 million cubic metres (304 million cubic yards) per second with a surface speed of nearly half a knot on average rising to one or two knots in places. This awesome flow makes the Amazon, at only 200,000 cubic metres (260,000 cubic yards) per second at flood, look puny.

In between the belts of westerly and easterly winds there is a zone where the atmosphere is set spinning in cyclones – rather like roller bearings between their inner and outer rings. These cyclones or depressions, which cause the bad weather characteristic of latitudes between 55°S and 70°S, can be seen in satellite pictures as cloud spirals ringing the continent. Since they process round the continent, depressions do not produce lasting current patterns to match in the water below them, but the two great embayments in the continent, the Ross Sea and the Weddell Sea, each contain eddies or gyres which in size and direction of spin correspond with atmospheric depressions.

The huge cauldron of the Weddell Sea is stirred by the easterly winds in the south and the westerlies at its northern edge in a clockwise gyre which dictates its ice distribution, biology and exploration. This gyre draws comparatively warm water at its north-east into a tongue of relatively ice-free water curving from the region of the South Sandwich Islands towards the south-west. This has provided the traditional access for ships into the Weddell Sea, which cannot be penetrated, except by powerful ice-breakers, directly from the north. At the head of the Weddell Sea is an enormous expanse of fixed ice, the Ronne-Filchner Ice Shelf. At its western margin the extremely cold easterly winds coming off the continent are deflected northwards by the mountains of the Antarctic Peninsula, rendering the Peninsula's east coast perennially frigid and ice-bound in contrast to the 'banana-belt' conditions that prevail to the west. North of the shelf-ice floats about one third of the entire pack-ice of the Antarctic. Some of this, together with icebergs, is deflected by the bent finger of the Peninsula and spins off in a plume from the north-west sector, which reaches across as far as the South Sandwich Islands.

Now we turn to the meridional circulation which is superimposed on that just described. At the ice edge, water is made denser not only by becoming colder, but also by being made more salty through the mixing-in of the brine which is produced when ice forms from seawater. Drift of the salt-free ice northwards ensures that the build-up of salinity is continuous. The dense, heavy water sinks and spreads northwards and eastwards over the sea floor. It can be recognized by its temperature and salinity characteristics and has been found to penetrate as far as 17° north of the equator in the Atlantic. It seems that bottom water is not produced all round the continent but mainly in the Weddell Sea and perhaps one other place, in the western Pacific sector. Little comes from the Ross Sea because a submarine ridge prevents the cold water from flowing out of it. Antarctic bottom water going north is replaced by water from the north which has been warmed as it crosses the equator and made more saline by mixing in of water from areas of high evaporation such as the Mediterranean. This is the warm deep layer already noted and it rises to the surface at about 65°S between the East and West Wind Drifts. There some of it goes south to be cooled and sink as Antarctic bottom water, the rest goes north as surface water which, as already mentioned, is freshened by melting ice and sinks beneath the sub-Antarctic surface water at the Convergence. Because the upwelling water is dispersed in two directions, this is known as the Antarctic Divergence. The amount of water brought into the Southern Ocean in this way has been estimated as 60 million cubic metres (78½ million cubic yards) per second – only about a quarter of the flow in the Circumpolar Current.

The two outstanding points in all this are firstly that the Southern Ocean is firmly and extensively linked by circulation patterns with the rest of the world ocean, and secondly that these circulation patterns are tied to those of the atmosphere. If Antarctica, or more particularly, perhaps, the Weddell Sea, were not there, our climate, sea communications and fisheries would be very different from what they are.

The Southern Ocean appears to have plenty of life in it.[73] This seems to be shown by the numbers of sea birds and seals, the once-abundant whales, and the patches of discoloured water that denote the presence of plankton. These appearances may be misleading since it is a characteristic of Antarctic animal life to congregate in crowds. It is a revealing exercise to calculate, for example, how much penguin there would be per square metre of sea surface if the population were spread out evenly over the whole Southern Ocean. It works out at 0.12 milligrams. Nevertheless, there is more life than one might expect in this unpromising environment, and the basis for it is the phytoplankton, the minute floating plants such as diatoms, which, like the green plants of the land, manufacture the organic materials of their cells from water and the carbon dioxide of the air by photosynthesis, using the energy of sunlight. The life processes of phytoplankton are slowed down by cold but even at freezing temperatures, other things being favourable, their numbers can double in three days. The mineral nutrients – nitrate, phosphate, silicate (diatoms have siliceous cell walls) and other inorganic materials – which they require are present in high concentration because the upwelling warm deep water has been enriched in its passage from the northern hemisphere by the decomposition of the remains of plankton organisms falling into it from above. Antarctic surface water, for example, has twice the concentrations of nitrate and phosphate found in the most fertile temperate seas. Light is available in the surface waters continuously in summer.

Were this all, the Southern Ocean should be a uniform dense soup of phytoplankton during the growing season. It is not; in some places phytoplankton is indeed dense and production rates as high as anywere in the sea, but over most of its area the Southern Ocean has rather sparse phytoplankton and low productivity. Why this should be is not altogether clear but turbulence seems to be an important factor. If the upper layers of the sea are mixed deeply by wind and storm, a phytoplankton cell may be carried back and forth between the sunlit surface and the darkness down below so that, on average, it will not get enough light to enable it to photosynthesize and grow. It is significant that the most phytoplankton production is found where the water column is stable and not mixed to any great depth. Phytoplankton may build up under ice and continue growing vigorously when the ice disappears, but growth stops as soon as the wind gets up and mixes the water.

Diatoms and other phytoplankton algae are grazed by the animal plankton (zooplankton). There is an enormous variety of species in the zooplankton, but the one which is most abundant south of the Convergence and which has come most to public notice is the krill, *Euphausia superba*, the staple diet of the baleen whales. This is a shrimp-like animal up to 5 centimetres (2 inches) in length. When not actively feeding, it collects in swarms with several thousand to the cubic metre, which, if near the surface, colour the water red. The individuals in these swarms show amazing co-ordination, swimming in parallel alignment and all altering course in the same instant, the whole swarm behaving as a living entity and changing its shape rather like a flight of starlings or an amoeba. Divers encountering a swarm are enchanted by the experience. This behaviour, however, makes things difficult for the marine biologist who has to study krill populations. A trawl may miss the swarms altogether or, if it goes among them, the krill may see it coming and, being agile creatures, get out of the way. However, acoustic scanning, a development of the echo sounder, seems to be giving an answer to the problem, and from the intensity of the reflected signals it is possible to gauge the density of swarms. By this means a super-swarm detected near Elephant Island was estimated to contain more than 2.5 million tonnes of krill.

Individual creatures may perhaps live for up to four years and breeding takes place in the summer. The eggs are released near the surface and then sink to about 2000 metres (6500 feet). There they are carried south in the warm, deep water so that, when they hatch and the larvae migrate upwards, they are able to ride back north in the surface water. In this way they maintain a distribution which does not go beyond the Convergence. Much remains to be learnt about krill. It becomes very elusive in winter but new evidence indicates that it then lives in the pack, feeding off the algae and other organisms that grow in the interstices between the ice-crystals, and that in the summer it switches to grazing on the planktonic algae.

South Georgia coastline (water-colour)

Krill is the key organism in the ecology of the Southern Ocean. Not only is it the food of the great whales, but penguins and other sea-birds feed on it and so do fish and crabeater seals, which incidentally are the most abundant seals in the world. Inevitably, bearing in mind that the whales which used to be there probably took something like 190 million tonnes of krill per year, man has thought to exploit this enormous stock of protein. When one considers that the annual catch of fish in the world amounts to only 70 million tonnes, it seems that krill could provide a substantial source of food for mankind. Catching krill by using sonar to locate swarms and an aimed mid-water trawl is easy and a catch of 8 to 12 tonnes an hour is average, although up to 35 tonnes in eight minutes gives the occasional *embarras de richesse*. Trawlers from the USSR started catching krill in 1962 and since then the Japanese and West Germans have joined in, fishing mainly around South Georgia. After harvesting nearly half a million tonnes in 1979–80, enthusiasm has waned and catches fallen off. Krill starts to go rancid quickly and so there must be some immediate preliminary processing. Krill paste and krill cheese products have a limited appeal, and krill meal is more expensive than fish meal as fodder with the additional disadvantage that the exoskeleton contains high concentrations of toxic fluoride.

In any case, it would be foolish to start taking large harvests of a key organism such as krill without knowing what the ecological consequences might be. Since the great reduction in whale stocks, populations of penguins and seals have increased and, possibly in the face of this increased competition for krill, the whales may have difficulty in re-establishing themselves. Large-scale fishing for krill by man might make the situation worse. Realizing the need for more knowledge before things went too far, the Scientific Committee for Antarctic Research, the international body responsible for co-ordinating work in the Antarctic, organized a multi-nation oceanographic programme called BIOMASS (Biological Investigations of Marine Antarctic Systems and Stocks) which started in 1977 and is now (1988) in the stage of analyzing and putting together the information it has collected. Any extensive exploitation of krill will in the future have a firmer scientific basis from which it can be regulated.

From the krill point of view, the whalebone or baleen whale is a fiendishly efficient agent of mass destruction and thoroughly deserving of extermination. The ingrained migratory habits of these whales bring them from the warmer waters, where they breed, to the areas in the Southern Ocean where krill are most abundant as the ice is retreating. They locate krill swarms by acoustic rather than visual means. Humpback whales have been observed to round up krill swarms; one method is to circle the patch of krill then to dive and come up vertically with open mouth to engulf the concentrated krill. Another is to swim below the surface and release a trail of air bubbles, then to swim up through the rising whorl of bubbles to take the krill which have been collected in it. The right whale characteristically feeds by skimming the surface with mouth open and head partially out of the water. The triangular, fringed baleen plates which grow from the whale's upper jaws form an efficient sieving system. In swallow-type feeding, a mouthful of food and water is taken in and then force-filtered through the baleen plates by contraction of grooves beneath chin and throat and raising the tongue in the mouth. The krill collected on the baleen is then swallowed – the throat of a whale is surprisingly small, only wide enough to admit a clenched fist and obviously unsuitable to take anything much larger than krill.

The baleen whales include the mighty blue whale, which can be as much as 30 metres (100 feet) in length and over 150 tonnes in weight, and the almost as big fin whale, both of which are now rare to the verge of extinction. The sei and minke whales, which are smaller but which have the same streamlined torpedo shape as the bigger ones, now bear the brunt of such whaling as still continues. The humpback and right whales are plumper in shape and slower in swimming, and it is these that were taken in the days when whales were pursued in small boats and harpooned by hand. The right whale was 'right' simply because it was the easiest to harpoon and continued to float when killed.

Besides the baleen whales there are toothed whales – the large sperm whale which lives on squid and the smaller killer whale which hunts in packs and eats anything from fish to elephant seals or bigger. It is the adult male sperm whale that appears in Antarctic waters, females and young males staying in temperate seas. Squid may be of such a size as to have tentacles 9 metres (30 feet) long, and the scars which are left by their suckers on the sperm whales' heads show that they are no easy prey. In pursuit of them, the whales dive to over 1000 metres (3300 feet) and may be down for over an hour. This presents many interesting problems for the physiologist, one of which we will touch on here because the extraordinary shape of the animal calls for an explanation.

A sperm whale has an enormous snout, amounting to a third of the total weight and a quarter of the length of the whale. It is in effect a ballast tank. The snout contains spermaceti oil, a clear liquid wax much valued in industry as a lubricant and detergent but of vital importance to the whale as a means of buoyancy regulation. Clearly, in order to dive with minimum effort to great depths the whale must adjust its buoyancy quickly and within fine limits. This seems to be achieved by changing the density of the spermaceti by regulating its temperature. The spermaceti organ is an efficient heat exchanger and the blood flowing through it can be cooled as necessary by being directed through capillaries in the skin of the head. Heat can also be lost by drawing cold water into the nasal passage via the blow-hole.

Calculations show that the necessary temperature changes can be achieved in a minute or two. Very neatly, since the head becomes heavier as the spermaceti is cooled and becomes denser, the whale is tipped into the diving position and conversely, as it is warmed up by redirection of the blood supply, the trim of the whale alters ready for ascent.[74]

Much of this information has been extracted directly from an ocean which is certainly the most fearsome that the world has to offer. *The Antarctic Pilot*, written by the hydrographer of the Navy with very British understatement, remarks 'Navigation in the area covered by this volume is rendered difficult by a number of considerations', which it goes on to list as sea-ice; sudden, violent and unpredictable changes in the weather; dangerous shoals rising precipitously from deep water; large seas and swells; instability of the compass; inadequate charts; absence of navigational aids; whiteouts; and entangling kelp. Ross's description of a storm in the Southern Ocean has already been given.

In spite of modern technology, the terror is still there as is seen in Phillip Law's account of a hurricane off Mac. Robertson Land. This struck the *Kista Dan*, a Danish ice-strengthened vessel of 1239 tonnes and 65 metres (215 feet) length on charter to the Australian National Antarctic Research Expedition, in March 1954 on her return from setting up Mawson Station. In six hours the wind rose from Force 8 (about 37 knots), through Force 12 (over 80 knots) to Force 14 (at which point no attempt is made to estimate wind speeds). The Auster aircraft lashed down on deck was the first casualty. Having unloaded stores at Mawson the ship was riding high in the water, which made it difficult to keep her head into the wind, and ballasting by pumping seawater into empty tanks was impossible because the pipes had frozen up. Soon the captain lost control of the ship and she broached to, lying on her port side, drifting helplessly, pounded by every breaking wave, and rolling from 10° to starboard to 60° or 70° to port. In the cabins everything that was not screwed down was flung continuously from one bulkhead to the other. An extreme roll dipped the ship's port side so far that the saloon portholes looked down into green water. There was a great danger that the ship would turn turtle and over a period of twelve hours it seemed that every roll would be her last. For much of the time it was night and pieces of ice as big as houses were around but could scarcely be picked out through the spume by searchlight or distinguished by radar from the general clutter of breaking waves. Although steering was impossible the engines were still running and when he could see icebergs the captain avoided them, by going full speed ahead or astern, as best he could. *Kista Dan* survived; after twenty-four hours the gale moderated to 60 knots, it was possible to prepare some simple warm food, and the crew could set to unblocking the frozen pipes so that some stability could be restored.[60(Law)]

Brunt Ice Shelf (oil)

However, the Southern Ocean is not invariably ferocious and it was unusually amenable when, in 1823, James Weddell, taking advantage of an absence of ice, penetrated into the sea which now bears his name and attained 3° further south than the redoubtable Cook. He was on a sealing expedition but he was a man of enquiring and observant mind and it had been agreed with the ships' owners that he could 'prosecute a search beyond the track of former navigators'. His vessels, the 160-tonne brig *Jane* and the 65-tonne cutter *Beaufoy*, were frail and unprotected against ice and the provisions they carried were inadequate for a prolonged voyage under Antarctic conditions. However, having got through the gales, fogs and fields of icebergs just south of the South Sandwiches, he ran into pleasant weather and ice-free waters and continued to 74°15'S, 34°16'W – to within about 150 nautical miles of the continental ice shelf. He did not see land and, prudently, decided to return:

> Our crews were naturally much disappointed at our ill success in not finding a southern land, as their interest in the voyage was to be a proportion of the cargo procured. In order, therefore, to reanimate them by acknowledging their merit, I expressed my approbation of their patient and orderly behaviour, and informed them that they were now to the southward of the latitude to which any former navigator had penetrated. Our colours were hoisted, and a gun was fired, and both crews gave three cheers. These indulgences, with an allowance of grog, dispelled their gloom, and infused a hope that fortune might yet be favourable.[75]

Serendipity played a part in this achievement – it was probably not until the summer of 1967 that the Weddell Sea was again so clear of ice – and although Weddell took the precaution of having his Chief Officer and two seamen swear to the truth of his log before the Commissioners of His Majesty's Customs, there were some who tried to follow him who became convinced he was a liar. But this is not to detract from the brilliance of the exploit; he recognized his chance and had the great gift of leadership to carry it through.

Others were not so lucky: the *Deutschland* was trapped in the Weddell Sea for nine months in 1912 before being released, while the *Antarctic* in 1902 and the *Endurance* in 1915 were both beset in the same sea area, crushed, and sank. In 1932 *Discovery II*, the first steel ship and only the seventh vessel of any sort to penetrate the Weddell Sea, was trapped and escaped only narrowly with a damaged rudder and holed fuel tank.

Today, with more powerful, ice-strengthened vessels and satellite imagery to show the distribution of ice, such contretemps are now more avoidable. All is not plain sailing, though, and it is still usually necessary to break through fields of moderate pack-ice. Ice-strengthened vessels such as RRS *Bransfield*, which makes an annual journey into the Weddell Sea to relieve the British Antarctic Survey station Halley, have bows cut away below the water line so that, on meeting an ice-floe, the ship rides up on top of it. Her weight will then crack the floe and in this manner she can cut her way through ice up to about 3 metres (10 feet) thick.

Techniques for getting through the pack-ice differ. Some masters bash with nicely-calculated brute force and one marvels at the strength of the ship that she can stand such knocks. Others favour the gentle approach: the bows are eased up on the ice and for a few moments nothing seems to happen, then cracks run out silently across the ice, the ship lurches, and begins to move forward slowly. When she is brought to a standstill again the ship goes astern and the process is repeated. If a ship is beset she may be able to wriggle free by shifting water from one ballast tank to another. Ice-breakers are a step beyond ice-strengthened vessels, both in thickness of plating and engine power. Being broad in the beam and without much of a keel they are uncomfortable ships in the open sea, rolling as much as 65° in the Roaring Forties on the way to Antarctica. The Soviet Antarctic flagship, the *Akademik Fedorov*, commissioned in 1987, has a 20,000 horse-power diesel-electric power plant that enables her to keep steadily under way in 1-metre (3-foot) thick level ice.

The ice is infinitely variable and there is a profusion of technical terms to describe it. Freezing usually begins by the formation of 'frazil ice', a slush with clumps of ice crystals in it. When the crystals and plates of ice form a thick layer at the surface, it gives the water a dull, matt appearance and is known as 'grease ice'. Crystals may grow to form a lattice at the surface under calm conditions; this is 'congelation ice'. As this skeletal ice and grease ice grows in thickness wave action shapes it into circular 'pancakes' which, through jostling against each other, come to have upturned edges. As the ice grows in thickness, it also changes in structure. For example, the surface may melt and the meltwater percolate downwards into the ice lattice, flushing out the brine left by the formation of ice crystals. Mechanical stress converts the spongy mass into hard ice. Ice crystals and stalactites form on the lower surface. In these sorts of ways sea-ice can grow in the course of two seasons to a thickness of 3 metres (10 feet) or so, when it reaches an equilibrium, losing as much by melting, sublimation and wind scour as it gains by addition of more ice. Wave action breaks floes up and the enormous pressures which develop when winds blow across large areas of pack-ice cause 'rafting' (in which one floe overrides another) in young ice, and ridges and hummocks in old ice. Pack-ice may be 'open', with plenty of water visible, or 'close', like a gigantic jig-saw puzzle in which some of the pieces do not quite fit together, giving 'leads' or channels between large areas of continuous ice.

Hazardous though it is for navigation, the pack-ice is fascinating and those not concerned with managing the ship are happy just to watch it pass for hours on end. The description which Edward Wilson gave in his *Discovery* diary cannot be bettered:

> The sky was grey with snow falling, the breakers were white on a dark grey sea and the ice only had its whiteness broken with the most exquisitely shaded blues and greens – pure blue, cobalt and pale emerald green and every mixture in between them ... And now we had loose ice all around us and here and there great frozen hummocks, where slabs the size of kitchen tables were thrown one on the other anyhow and so frozen, with every hollow and crack and crevice a perfect miracle of blue and green light.[76]

All these colours are produced by interactions of the substance water, either as liquid or ice, and sunlight.[77] The drops of water making up a cloud can be so densely packed as to act as a nearly opaque white body and reflect back most of the light received from the sun. To those below, a continuous cloud cover acts as a neutral filter and its greyness is mirrored by the sea surface. If such reflections are avoided then the colour of the water itself is seen. Water is not completely colourless but absorbs light more at the violet and red ends of the spectrum, being most transparent to blue. Deep pure water with nothing in it to reflect light back would appear black because it would absorb all the light penetrating into it. The most transparent seawater in the world, which has been found in the Antarctic, gets near this. Much of the Southern Ocean contains little suspended matter, such as plankton, to scatter and reflect light back to the surface and approximates to pure water, appearing a deep indigo blue. Such light as is returned to the surface passes through a great thickness of water and has all other wavelengths but blue removed.

A great thickness of pure ice would behave similarly. Icebergs contain glacial ice – hard and transparent – and white ice, which, containing abundant air bubbles, reflects diffusely most of the light which falls on it. Even glacial ice has a few bubbles and crystal surfaces which reflect and refract so that the light, bouncing backwards and forwards through the ice, has a long effective path length and consequently, when it emerges from even comparatively small pieces, is blue. Light may be conducted, as along an optical fibre, so that crevices are luminous with sapphire light. Sunlight contains a large proportion of yellow light and, if it is reflected back through a moderate thickness of water, the reflecting object is seen as green because of the combination of the blue of the water with unabsorbed yellow from sunlight. Thus white ice below the water appears emerald green and so does ice containing moderate amounts of bubbles. Sometimes, however, large pieces of ice, even whole icebergs, appear bottle-green, making a startling contrast

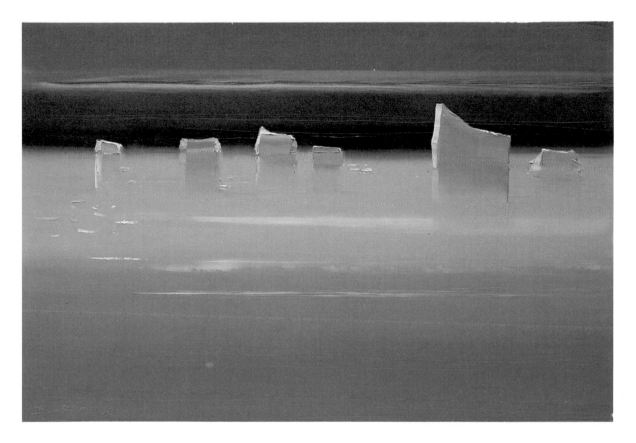

Icebergs, Weddell Sea (oil)

with adjacent white ice. This colour appears intrinsic rather than dependent on lighting conditions. Such ice has contaminants, such as organic particles in it, but it is not clear whether the colour originates from these or some special structure of the ice itself.

The icescape changes with the light and we may again turn to Wilson's diary, this time from *Terra Nova* days, for a description of the scene when the sun is low on the horizon.

> One looks out upon endless fields of broken ice, all violet and purple in the low shadows, and all gold and orange and rose-red on the broken edges which catch the light, while the sky is emerald green and salmon pink, and these two beautiful tints are reflected in the pools of absolutely still water which here and there lie between the ice-floes. Now and again one hears a penguin cry out in the stillness near at hand or far away, and then, perhaps, he appears in his dress tail coat and white waistcoat suddenly upon an ice floe from the water – and catching sight of the ship runs curiously towards her, crying out in amazement as he comes, from time to time, but only intensifying the wonderful stillness and beauty of the whole fairy-like scene as the golden glaring sun in the south just touches the horizon and begins again to gradually rise without having really set at all.[78]

The penguin mentioned here is the adelie. Often a dozen or so are encountered together on the pack-ice, seemingly commenting with bewilderment and admiration on the astonishing object which has suddenly crashed its way into their world. Only if the floe on which they stand is rocked by the passage of the vessel do they take to the water in panic. The more solitary emperor penguin regards the manifestation of a ship with dignified reserve. Flighted birds in the pack-ice include various petrels – snow, Antarctic and Wilson's. The first are most attractive birds – small, pure white with black bill, eyes and feet – and, seen against a dark sea, they look like paper cutouts. Crabeater seals, lying around like huge slugs on the floes, are only mildly interested in what is going on unless actually tipped off into the sea. The occasional whale is also to be seen but in the late 1970s one might encounter as many whale-catchers as whales in a passage through the Weddell Sea.

The diatoms which provide the basis for this life are more in evidence here than they usually are in the open ocean, old floes tipped over by the passage of a ship showing a yellow stain in the ice on their undersides. This was noticed by Cook and other early explorers who supposed it was earth picked up when the ice was formed on land. Ross, with Mount Erebus in view, thought it must be volcanic ash. It was Hooker, his assistant surgeon, who looked at the yellow material under the microscope and saw that it consisted of organisms of some sort. He preserved samples which were later sent to the eminent German zoologist Ehrenberg who described and illustrated the numerous different sorts accurately, but missed the significant point because he thought they were animals, not plants. Later, Hooker decided that they must be plants and, realizing how widespread and abundant they were, came to the conclusion that here were the primary producers of food in the oceans. The basic fact of biological oceanography had been established from observations in the Antarctic.

Dominating the scene in the Southern Ocean are the icebergs. Their dominance is physical as well as visual; responding to currents at depth rather than to wind, they plough irresistibly through floes and brash ice (fragments). The characteristic Antarctic berg is tabular with a flat top and vertical sides rising around 30 metres (100 feet) above the water and having up to ten times that amount submerged. The average tabular berg is as much as half a kilometre (quarter of a mile) in diameter, but a few are tremendous, 160 kilometres (100 miles) or so in length. One which broke away from the Ross Ice Shelf in 1987 was almost the size of Cyprus. Drift is at the rate of 8–16 kilometres (5–10 miles) a day, and most do not survive a summer season once they have reached the open sea.

Disintegration takes place by the mutually assisting processes of melting and breakage by the mechanical stress of wave action. Weak spots such as crevasses and softer ice are eroded first so that, underwater, a tabular berg becomes highly irregular. Sooner or later it becomes unbalanced and tilts or tips right over. The result is the berg of 'romantick' shape which beguiled Captain Cook. Caves, arches, flutings, pinnacles, turrets and castellations

'Bergy bits' off the Inaccessible Islands, South Orkney group. Lithograph after E. Goupil. (d'Urville, *Atlas Pittoresque*, 1841–5, vol. 1, plate 27: courtesy of the Scott Polar Research Institute)

abound and inevitably there is sometimes a statuesque bit, often resembling Queen Victoria. Whether gleaming against a dark sea, looming mysteriously as a blue-grey bulk out of the mist, or silhouetted against a stormy sky, icebergs are always worth contemplating. On a calm day it is tempting to explore their grottoes and basins more closely, but once having seen an iceberg suddenly topple or disintegrate one suppresses this inclination.

The fragments are called 'bergy bits' if sizeable, or 'brash ice' if they are smaller, but the ultimate end product, of course, is liquid water.[79] A large iceberg represents a huge amount of water purer than average distilled water, so the thought arises that here is a possible solution to the problems of water shortages in the southern hemisphere. Icebergs can be towed – small ones were brought from Alaska to San Francisco to alleviate water shortages in the nineteenth century – and calculation suggests that a 1-kilometre ($\frac{1}{2}$-mile) berg towed to southern Australia would be economically worthwhile. One problem would be to identify structurally sound bergs that would not disintegrate during the journey, and another would be to select the point of origin in relation to currents so as to reduce to a minimum the time spent in warm waters. All in all, it seems unlikely that Saudi Arabia will ever benefit from Antarctic icebergs (see page 202).

Icebergs may carry rocks – the sight of a large boulder, supported unseen by a bracket of ice from a nearby berg, floating buoyantly in the waves is one of the most flabbergasting I have encountered – and these eventually drop off to litter the ocean floor. Such rocks are a certain indication of land, but the continent to the south mostly lies behind enormous shelves of ice. Before that is reached, scattered here and there in the Southern Ocean are lonely outposts of land, assailed by ferocious seas and winds and mostly fog- and ice-bound – the peri-Antarctic islands.

Argentine islands – rock and icescape (water-colour)

The sea freezing (water-colour)

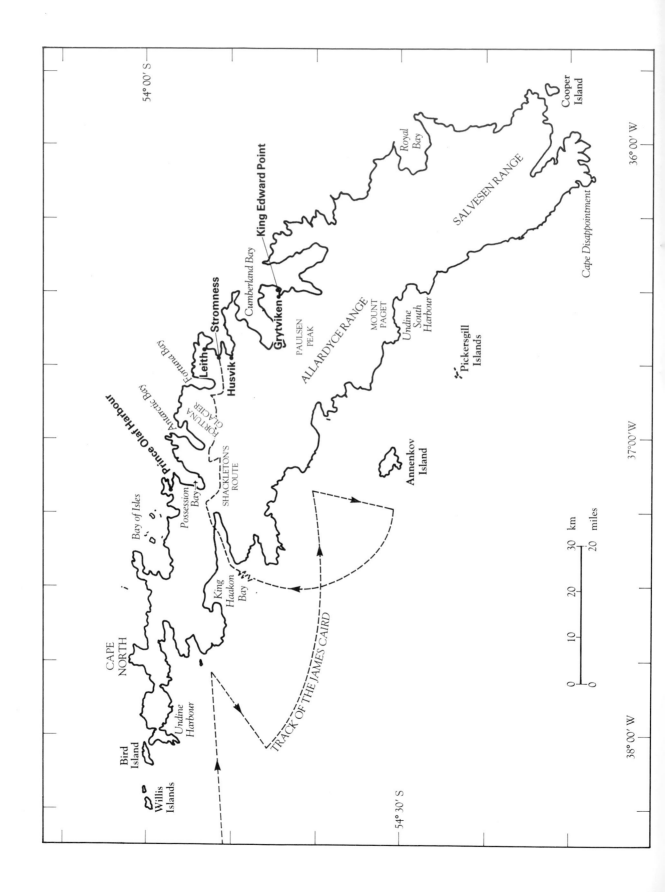

54° 00' S

Cooper
Island

*Royal
Bay*

SALVESEN RANGE

Cumberland Bay

King Edward Point

Cape Disappointment

Stromness

Leith

Grytviken

Fortuna Bay

Husvik

PAULSEN
PEAK

MOUNT
PAGET

ALLARDYCE RANGE

Antarctic Bay

*Undime
South
Harbour*

FORTUNA
GLACIER

Prince Olaf Harbour

*Possession
Bay*

*Pickersgill
Islands*

SHACKLETON'S
ROUTE

Bay of Isles

*Annenkov
Island*

CAPE
NORTH

*King
Haakon
Bay*

**Bird
Island**

*Undime
Harbour*

*Willis
Islands*

TRACK OF THE JAMES CAIRD

54° 30' S

38° 00' W   37° 00' W   36° 00' W

0   10   20   30   km
0   10   20   miles

Chapter Five

The Island of South Georgia

T HE ISLE OF MAN, off the coast of Britain, is as far north as South Georgia is south, yet on the one frosts are infrequent and sub-tropical shrubs flourish, while the other has glaciers and permanent snow fields. The reason for this extraordinary difference is that the Isle of Man is bathed by water from the Gulf Stream whereas South Georgia lies south of the Antarctic Convergence where it is surrounded all the year round by water only a little above freezing point. As a result the island is truly Antarctic. For various reasons, however, South Georgia is different from the other peri-Antarctic islands and deserves special notice.

As the most northerly of the Antarctic's outposts, South Georgia was the first to be discovered and has seen more of the extremes of human behaviour than other places in the region. It was most probably first sighted by Antoine de la Roche, a London merchant, when, on returning from a voyage to Peru in 1675, he was carried off course after rounding the Horn. However, it was Cook who, in 1775, first fixed its position accurately and made the first landing. He did not find it prepossessing and in an often quoted passage described Possession Bay, where he landed, in the following terms:

> The inner parts of the country were not less savage and horrible. The wild rocks raised their lofty summits, till they were lost in the clouds, and the valleys lay covered with everlasting snow. Not a tree was to be seen, nor a shrub even big enough to make a toothpick.[80]

The Island of South Georgia showing Shackleton's route

Rather artlessly, immediately after dismissing his find as 'not worth the

117

discovery', he went on to name it 'the Isle of Georgia in honour of his Majesty'. Worthless or not, he reported that the islands had numerous fur seals and, as we have already seen, this was sufficient to attract further visitors. Sealing on South Georgia probably began with a visit from the *Lord Hawkesbury* out of London in 1787. In 1801, when the American sealing captain Edmund Fanning himself obtained 57,000 fur seal skins on the island, there were seventeen other sealing vessels there also and he estimated the total number of skins taken as 112,000. The seals could not withstand this onslaught and soon after Fanning's visit it became uneconomic to make voyages to South Georgia for fur. Elephant seals were also killed, for their oil, and this trade lasted a little longer before in turn collapsing. Thereafter, stocks both of fur and elephant seals recovered somewhat and sealing was resumed intermittently, finally petering out in the early years of the twentieth century.

Relics of this phase of South Georgia's history are scattered about the island; try-pots in which blubber was rendered down, caves with the remains of hearths in them, graveyards – one skeleton showing evidence of a bullet through the skull – and wrecks of boats. One of the few written records left by a South Georgian sealer is a book, published in 1844, with the following informative title:

A Narrative of the Life, Travels and Sufferings of Thomas W. Smith, Comprising an Account of his Early Life, Adoption by the Gypseys, his Travels during Eighteen Voyages to Various Parts of the World, during which he was Shipwrecked Five Times, thrice on a Desolate Island near the South Pole, once on the coasts of England and once on the coast of Africa . . . Written by Himself.

The 'Desolate Island near the South Pole' was South Georgia, to which Smith devotes three chapters. His sufferings included not only shipwreck, near shipwreck, starvation, and sleeping in the open in intense cold, but destitution through bankruptcy of the ship's owner when he returned to London. It is perhaps not surprising that he makes little comment on the beauties of South Georgia, but the sealers evidently managed to preserve their sense of humour. When some ice on which Smith and his companions were encamped for the night broke up, they launched their boats with great difficulty, then:

Having succeeded in this we rowed off at a little distance from the shore and laid on our oars, while we breakfasted by taking some raw pork and biscuit and a glass of spirit, which was then thought to be essential to renovate our spirits. We recommenced our search along the frightful and dangerous iron-bound shore and proceeded until late in the evening, at which time we arrived at the east branch of Tamering Bay. When there we rowed to a strong beach, near which was a half-moon cavern dry and free from snow. Here we took up our lodgings for the night. After supper, while on the point of retiring to our beds, which were composed of the huge round stones, the boatswain made some remarks respecting our present condition when contrasted with the most affluent in England, and jocosely took a white pigeon which we had taken, and plucking some of its feathers gave two to each individual, advising us to put them under us and sleep on them, that on some future day we might say that we had slept on feathers while engaging in sealing on the coast of Georgia.[81]

The 'white pigeon' must have been the sheathbill, *Clionis alba*, a common scavenger on South Georgia, and which does, indeed, resemble a pigeon.

In 1904 Carl Larsen, the enterprising Norwegian whaling captain who had taken part in two exploring expeditions in the Antarctic Peninsula area and seen the abundance of whales in the Southern Ocean, set up a whaling station on South Georgia with capital from Argentina. By this time the invention of the explosive harpoon and the development of fast whale-catchers enabled whalers to go after the big blue and fin whales of the Antarctic. Others followed Larsen and the Government of the Falkland Island

Possession Bay, South Georgia, 17 January 1775; copper engraving after W. Hodges. (Cook, *A Voyage towards the South Pole*, 1777, vol. 2, p.212)

Dependencies stepped in to regulate matters. One of the old school of sealers, Captain B. D. Cleveland, master of the brig *Daisy* of New Bedford, Massachusetts, visited South Georgia in 1912–13, just as this new phase was beginning. The *Daisy* was a sailing ship with no auxiliary power and besides taking seals hunted whales in the old way, from a whale-boat with hand-held harpoons. For a whaler she met a premature and ignominious end; in the First World War she was used as a merchant vessel and, springing a leak, was burst asunder by the swelling of the cargo of beans she was carrying, sinking in the Atlantic after only forty-four years service. On the *Daisy* on her visit to South Georgia was a young naturalist, Robert Cushman Murphy, who had married only four months before the beginning of the voyage. For his bride he wrote his delightful *Logbook for Grace*, which gives us a picture of South Georgia as it was then. On his first landing he encountered the full awfulness of whaling:

> The tiny, land-locked haven of Grytviken, or King Edward Cove, finally greeted us through the sense of smell even before we had rounded the point that hides its entrance. The odor of very stale whale then increased amain as we entered the cove, which might be likened to a great cauldron so filled with the rotting flesh and macerated bones of whales that they not only bestrew its bottom but also thickly encrust its rim to the farthest high water mark. At the head of the cove, below a pointed mountain, we could see the whaling station, its belching smoke, several good-sized steamers, and a raft of whale carcasses. Fragments of entrails and other orts of whales were floating out to sea.
>
> Near the entrance of the cove was a substantial frame building flying the Union Jack. Toward this we headed and, upon landing (I first), we were courteously greeted by a gentleman in tweeds who introduced himself as Mr. James Innes Wilson, His Majesty's Stipendiary Magistrate, representing the Government of the Falkland Islands in the Dependency of South Georgia.[82]

Captain Cleveland was puzzled and troubled by these new developments, recalling 'the South Georgia of former years as quite outside the human and lawful world.'

> He had called on His Majesty's Magistrate, and his worst fears were confirmed. Sovereign government functions at South Georgia; law and regulation have reached an island that was formerly the Old Man's personal property; King George is being nasty to him. There are rules about what size and sex of sea elephants he may kill. There are port charges in Cumberland Bay and a fee for his sealing permit. Worst of all, in accordance with a statute in force only since last month, an export license is required

for the sea elephant oil that he will take away with him. What is the world coming to, when a peaceful whaler and sealer can't go about its business without being pestered and bled white by a gang of ___, ___, ___ limejuicers![82]

It hardly needs to be added that he ignored the rules and conveniently forgot to obtain clearance at King Edward Point before departure.

In the 'gold-rush' days there were six major whaling stations on South Georgia. These were largely self-sufficient with not only plant for converting whales into oil and fertilizers, but their own workshops, pigsties, hospital, cinema, football ground and, at Grytviken, a church. This last has had to yield its distinction of being the most southerly in the world to 'The Chapel of the Snows' at the US base at McMurdo, but it can still claim to have the most southerly peal of bells. Life on South Georgia thus had its comforts – for some at least. Murphy was inclined to sarcasm in describing it:

When we entered the residence of Captain Larsen and his staff, our illusions of the rude Antarctic were shattered for the moment by luxuriant palms and blossoming plants that banked walls and casements. A glance through the window of the billiard room showed that 'the maid was in the garden, hanging up the clothes,' but we afterwards learned that she was the only woman in all South Georgia. Still farther within this crude abode, or igloo, we were shown into a salon containing a piano, a conservatory of plants, singing canaries, and several portraits, including one of King Haakon, of Norway. Every evidence of hardship, what?

Well, to go on with my tale of hardship, the meal was served by only one butler and it comprised not more than eight courses with beer. An excellent brand of Havana cigars was passed round at the end, and I was almost sorry that I do not smoke. It calls for a good constitution to endure this antarctic fare – otherwise a man could die of gout.

The existence of the whaling stations made South Georgia a good jumping-off place for further south, and the German *Deutschland* expedition under Dr Wilhelm Filchner and the *Endurance* expedition under Shackleton, by then Sir Ernest, both made it their forward base. *The Endurance* stayed at Grytviken for a month before sailing south-east on 5 December 1914 to her destruction 2400 kilometres (1500 miles) away in the Weddell Sea. On 20 May 1916 three worn-out, ragged and utterly filthy men descended from the mountains to the west behind the whaling station of Stromness. Two boys took to their heels at the sight of them and the station manager, who had known Shackleton well but presumed him dead, had to ask who they were. The reply, 'My name is Shackleton', is said to have brought tears to the eyes of even those hard-bitten whalers.

Sea-ice (water-colour)

Ten days earlier, the *James Caird* had beached in King Haakon Bay on the south-west coast of South Georgia after her epic voyage across 1300 appalling kilometres (800 miles) of sea from Elephant Island. This coast faces the full blast of the prevailing winds and offers no shelter, but to sail round the island to the more hospitable north-east coast where the whaling stations were was beyond the remaining strengths of either men or boat. The nearest whaling station, at Prince Olaf Harbour, was actually less than 16 kilometres (10 miles) away overland but Shackleton was unaware of this and made instead for Stromness 35 kilometres (22 miles) away as the crow flies. The then unmapped mountains and glaciers which form the spine of South Georgia presented a hurdle certainly as formidable as the sea that they had just crossed but, after a few days rest and a wait for good weather, Shackleton with two companions, Crean and Worsley, set out leaving the others sheltering beneath the *James Caird*, in what they called Peggotty Camp, to be rescued later.

The *James Caird* approaching King Haakon Bay, South Georgia, May 1916; oil painting by Norman Wilkinson. (Courtesy of Dulwich College)

A British Services expedition which retraced Shackleton's route in 1964 experienced great difficulties, including being held up for a day and a half by a storm and nearly losing three men in an avalanche, in spite of starting fresh

and having abundant food and the best of equipment. Shackleton knew that the only hope for him was to keep going and, with several detours, some retracing of steps and taking hair-raising risks, they did the journey in thirty-six hours with scarcely any rest. Luck or divine providence – and Shackleton had no doubt that it was the latter – but they had hit a window of fine weather which let them through. Before or after and they would undoubtedly have perished. At 6.30 a.m. on 20 May, while they were still groping through unknown country, Shackleton thought he heard a steam whistle from a whaling factory. If he really had heard it he knew it would be repeated at 7 a.m. to call the men to work. As the three of them waited with eyes riveted to their chronometer it came precisely on time – the first sound from the human world they had heard for seventeen months. That was the moment of supreme satisfaction in achievement, although sinking into a hot bath a few hours later must have been almost as sweet.[41]

Shackleton died at Grytviken six years later of a coronary thrombosis aboard his ship the *Quest* at the beginning of his next expedition south. He lies in the little cemetery at Grytviken in company with whalers and surrounded by the magnificent peaks of the Allardyce Range. Storm battered wreaths of artificial flowers and other tributes left by visiting ships cover his grave.

At this time Grytviken and the other whaling stations on South Georgia were booming. The Colonial Office, remembering the collapse of the Greenland and Spitsbergen whale fisheries, realized that something had to be done to conserve stocks in the face of the slaughter that was going on. Regulations were made to restrict the number of whaling stations, to protect female whales accompanied by calves, and to ensure utilization of the whole whale carcass and not just the best bits.

Despite the First World War being at its height, a committee was appointed in London to consider what further measures might be taken, and in 1920 it made its report. The outcome was that a tax on each barrel of oil was used to fund investigations to provide a scientific basis for the industry. It was this report that made a recommendation that the fisheries around the Falkland Islands should be developed and one wonders how different things might have been in the South Atlantic had notice been taken then of what the scientists had to say. However, for the rest, the report was acted upon and Scott's old ship the *Discovery*, which had been doing duty as a store ship with the Hudson's Bay Company in the Canadian Arctic, was taken south again to carry out oceanographic observations. She was joined by a specially built vessel, the *William Scoresby*, named after an Arctic whaling captain who not only achieved legendary fame in that capacity but was a pioneer in Arctic marine science and the study of magnetism. Captain Scoresby became a Fellow of the Royal Society, and later, after obtaining a Doctorate of

Divinity, was a successful vicar in an unruly industrial parish.

Between these two vessels thousands of oceanographic observations were made. The oceanographer likes his observations to be synoptic, that is to say, made simultaneously over the whole area of study. To get as near to this ideal as possible over the 26,000 square kilometres (10,000 square miles) of sea that it was necessary to cover around South Georgia, the two ships occupied twenty-nine stations in five and a half days of often stormy weather, taking 370 water samples and 307 plankton net hauls. The scientists worked continuously for two periods of twenty-four hours each, with only a few hours of sleep in between. Probably for sheer intensity of work this has never been equalled on any other oceanographic cruise. Friendly competition between the two vessels helped considerably towards this achievement. Besides these studies, designed to determine the distribution of the krill on which whales feed, there were cruises to mark whales so that their migrations might be followed. Accurate charts of the South Sandwich, the South Orkney and the South Shetland Islands, as well as of South Georgia itself, were made and in the course of two circumnavigations of the Antarctic continent the position of the Antarctic Convergence was plotted. The Discovery Investigations reports fill some 1.5 metres (5 feet) of shelf.[42]

All this was fine but the development in the 1920s of factory ships on which the entire processing of whales could be done while on the high seas enabled whalers to move outside the jurisdiction of the Colonial Government. The remorseless hunting intensified but land-based factories such as that at Grytviken, after reaching a peak when almost 8000 whales were brought into South Georgia in the mid-1920s, gradually fell into disuse. In the heyday of Grytviken the population, which was mostly Norwegian, rose to as much as 700 and some of the officers of the whaling stations and of the neighbouring British administration brought their wives and even children. One of these wives, Nan Brown, wrote a book, *Antarctic Housewife*.[85] She enjoyed her sojourn in the tough and overwhelmingly male environment and gave a picture of Grytviken as a cheerful village-like place with a higher than average proportion of colourful characters. Soon it was to become a ghost town. The factories of South Georgia closed one by one and all whaling activities ceased by 1967. The government, not wanting to maintain an expensive administrative presence but unwilling to leave the island unoccupied, then encouraged the British Antarctic Survey to set up a base at King Edward Point.

Out of a naval operation, code-named 'Tabarin', in the Antarctic during the Second World War there grew the Falkland Islands Dependencies Survey, an organization charged with surveying and scientific investigation in the area of Antarctica claimed by Britain. When in 1961 such territorial claims were put in abeyance under the Antarctic Treaty, the name was changed to

British Antarctic Survey (BAS) but the acronym 'Fids' survives as a label for the men working for the survey.

An attempt must be made to describe these successors to the whalers although their characteristically individual personalities make this difficult. Appearance is easiest: most are bearded and a well-worn and faded green or orange anorak, a woolly hat knitted by girlfriend or mother, and an expensive camera are standard dress. There is also a general similarity in speech laced with an esoteric vocabulary of naval slang compounded with Fids-invented words. Thus to sleep in one's bed is to 'gonk' in one's 'pit', bits of dirt on a photograph are 'blegs' on a 'grip', and 'splode' is another word for thingummy or what-not.

Most Fids are in their early twenties and under contract for three years. They include builders, cooks, doctors, diesel mechanics, radio operators, meteorologists, divers, field assistants and research scientists, but the tradition is that everyone must be prepared to turn his hand to anything. If stores need unloading on to a rocky shore without quay or jetty then all hump packing-cases and roll oil-drums from a heaving scow into safety well above the high tide mark. All must help with washing up and take an occasional turn in the kitchen to give the cook a day off. If there is an accident and no doctor is available then someone has to do something; in one such emergency a biologist, following instructions over the radio, had to remove a damaged eye – and he did it successfully. The supreme jack-of-all-trades is the base commander, who may not be much older than his fellow Fids. In addition to being responsible for organizing the work of the base he is sworn in as a Magistrate before he takes up his duties and has to act as Postmaster, Registrar of Births, Marriages and Deaths, Coroner, Deputy Receiver of Wrecks and Deputy Controller of Customs. On more than one occasion he has had to be Her Majesty's plenipotentiary in the face of armed aggression. Even if the scientific work of the Survey were valueless – which it certainly is not – the training it gives in self-reliance would be well worth the expense.[83]

South Georgia has so far been of most interest to the BAS biologists.[84] Its inshore waters are rich in plant and animal life, including the young stages of *Notothenia rossii*, a toothsome fish that is now in danger of over-exploitation in the waters surrounding the island. The plant life on land is luxuriant by Antarctic standards and includes *Acaena magellanica*, a handsome relative of the British salad burnet, with hooked fruits having a special affinity for Fids' regulation issue trousering and socks (the latter being rendered useless), and *Paradiochloa flabellata*, tussock grass, an excellent fodder plant. The few flowering plants, together with the mosses and lichens, provide brilliant patches of colour in sheltered spots. There is much of scientific interest in relating the growth and habit of these plants to the micro-climates of the places in which they occur.

Among the larger animals are rats, introduced accidentally by the whalers and damaging to the bird life. Another introduction, a deliberate one, is the reindeer, which finds the vegetation to its liking and flourishes. Fortunately the reindeer are confined to restricted areas by glaciers and so do not affect the ecology of the whole island. Birds – penguins of four sorts, albatrosses, petrels, cormorants and, surprisingly, a species of pipit and a pin-tail duck are abundant. These birds are mostly unafraid of man and submit without too much fuss to being weighed or having radio transmitters attached to them so that their foraging behaviour can be monitored. Elephant and fur seal populations have recovered. Intensive studies of both birds and seals are carried out from a small base on an island off the north of South Georgia to which the name Bird Island was given by Captain Cook 'on accou^t of the vast number that were upon it'. This is still true; it is estimated that on its 150 hectares (370 acres) there are 175,000 breeding pairs of macaroni penguins and 500,000 breeding pairs of dove prions.

On landing on Bird Island, the first intimation one may have of the presence of wandering albatrosses could be prints in the snow of a webbed foot much larger than a human hand. Looking up, the wind-swept, tussock-covered hillside is seen to be dotted with widely-spaced white specks, each a nesting albatross. The nest is a tussock clump worn and padded with grass to a comfortable shape and the bird sits on it regally. She has a breast of the purest white, black wings and the only remonstrance she makes if approached too closely is to clap her beak. The ever-resourceful Fid has been known to ensure that his lunch-time beer is at an acceptable temperature by slipping the can under an eggless but brooding albatross, which accepts it trustingly as a correctly sized, if strangely shaped, egg.

The wandering albatross is the largest of all flying sea-birds, weighing up to 10 kilograms (22 pounds) and with a wing span of 2.5–3 metres (8–10 feet). It has to make an undignified crash-landing and, once on the ground, has difficulty in getting airborne again. Consequently the nesting site is chosen to make take-off as easy as possible. Back in the air its flight is seemingly effortless, making use of updraughts with minimum movement of its stiffly-held, narrow wings. In this way, carried by the westerlies, it circles the globe and journeys of over 5000 kilometres (3000 miles) in ten days have been recorded. An escorting albatross planing around a ship is a signal that it has reached southern waters, but these birds do not go further than about 56°S. The superstitions about the albatross publicized by Coleridge may be taken symbolically[86], but its real menace to a sailor is if he goes overboard, when the bird will attack, going first for the eyes.

The chicks, one per nest, are hatched in late summer and after four or five weeks of brooding are left on their own while both parents forage for squid and fish. Sitting urbanely on its throne, well insulated by thick white woolly down and layers of fat, with no predators to molest it and being fed at intervals, it faces the winter out. No predators, that is, except for the occasional man; Shackleton and his companions after landing on South Georgia had compunction in taking these chicks but found they made a tasty and sustaining stew. The young birds spend several years at sea before returning to their native islands to breed. There is an elaborate ritual of courtship dancing and nest-building which may be gone through on two or three subsequent years before there is any tangible outcome, but the partnerships which are established are lasting ones. Mature birds breed only every other year and may live to be fifty.

The other bird which must be mentioned here is the king penguin. This does not nest on Bird Island but there are rookeries containing thousands of them in the fjords of South Georgia. The king penguin is almost as dignified and even more handsome than its larger relative, the emperor. Its white shirt front is flushed with orange-yellow beneath its throat. Its back and the upper sides of its flippers are dark grey and its bill and patches behind each eye are a brilliant orange. Like the emperor penguin, the king penguin does not build a nest but incubates its single egg balanced on top of its feet and covered with a warm fold of belly. Hence it needs a fairly flat site for nesting so that it can shuffle around without unbalancing the egg. In the rookery the nesting patches are marked out by radial splashes of white excrement and spaced evenly so as to be just out of pecking range of each other. Sad to say, this splendid bird was once taken in large numbers for its blubber and plumage, but it is now beginning to recover its former numbers on the more northerly Antarctic islands – further south it is replaced by the emperor. Now its main predator is the sea leopard.

A third bird, the giant petrel, has to be given attention out of scientific impartiality rather than for any attractive features it possesses. Commonly known as the 'stinker', it feeds on carrion and, given the chance, will gorge to the extent that it has to be sick before it can fly again. Stinkers were always around amid the blood and guts of the whaling station or sealing beach. If one wishes to approach a nesting bird it is best to poke it first with a long stick, so as to be out of range of its squirted vomit, and wait until it has expended its nauseating ammunition. Like many petrels, it ejects a copious yellow stomach oil with a smell that clings to clothes however often they are washed.

Bird Island is noted for its fur seals almost as much as for its birds. After the fur seal had been hunted almost to extinction in the nineteenth century, a few evidently survived on the Willis Islands, a group of steep-sided islands and rocks protected by tide-rips and confused seas, and thence colonized neighbouring Bird Island, where by 1956 the population had reached

12,000. Even ten years later the fur seal was a great rarity on other peri-Antarctic islands, the occasional individual causing great excitement and much clicking of cameras. In the absence of hunting and with less competition from whales for their staple food, krill, fur seals have now multiplied spectacularly and become almost, be it whispered, a pest. There are probably about a million of them on South Georgia and they are becoming numerous in the South Orkneys. The bull seals, which may be nearly 2 metres (6½ feet) in length and weigh about 140 kilograms (300 pounds), establish territories in early spring, battling for the most favoured spots, with the younger and less experienced ending up on the more inadequate rocks or remote places in the tussock. Perhaps they have a folk-memory of seal-hunters, but certainly one is well advised to keep clear of the bulls, which are aggressive and fast-moving. They are joined by their harems of the much smaller females a few weeks later, pups being born shortly afterwards and mating taking place shortly after that. So crowded are the colonies that on Bird Island it has been found necessary to erect walk-ways on scaffolding above them so that zoologists can carry out their studies in relative safety without disturbing the seals.

Investigations of the foraging habits of the seals and sea-birds in the seas around South Georgia has revealed that although several of them share the same prey – krill – they do not compete with each other because their fishing techniques and foraging ranges are so different. Thus the gentoo and macaroni penguins both catch krill individually by diving and pursuit down to 100 metres (330 feet) or so in the depth range where large krill concentrations are found even during the day. They both have similar swimming speeds, of about 1.9 metres (6 feet) per second, but whereas the gentoo goes foraging every day within a range of around 30 kilometres (20 miles), the macaroni takes longer trips out to 115 kilometres (70 miles), so that their hunting grounds to not overlap.[87] Fur seals, which also live on krill and also have a diving limit of about 100 metres (330 feet), may compete with these birds for food. By attaching small radio transmitters to females and following them from tracking stations on two of the main Bird Island peaks, it was found that the usual foraging trip was out to 15–20 kilometres (9–12 miles) and took from twelve to sixteen hours overall. Since the seals and the penguins favour different kinds of ground for breeding, they are able to co-exist.

While the natural world readjusts itself after the ravages of man the hunter, his artefacts on South Georgia fall into decay. The whalers had pulled out leaving machinery and stores. Their stations would be of great interest to industrial archaeologists but weather and vandalism by crews of the many vessels which now call in at South Georgian harbours are rapidly taking their toll. Nevertheless, they still have their fascination, not least for the painter; David Smith recorded his impressions in his diary as follows:

Hamburg Glacier, South Georgia (water-colour)

The shapes, colours and textures of the buildings give an endless variety of compositions. Rusting steam winches, twisted girders, blocks and tackle, machinery of all kinds, still retaining among the rust some of the original paint, provide endless subjects for brush and camera. Artists seem to revel in the patina of surfaces caused by decay and the ravages of time. If the great French artist Utrillo had had the opportunity of coming here he would surely have enjoyed painting this place as much as he enjoyed painting the flaking walls of his beloved Montmartre. For the artists, the multitudinous layers of flaking paint give qualities of surface and texture impossible to imagine. The colours originally applied to ships and buildings are now drained of their former brashness by wind, rain and snow, and are transformed into subtle, delicate tints. When these objects are cloaked in snow the pictorial result is pure magic.

To the ravages of time have been added those of war. The arrival of scrap merchants on South Georgia in itself was to be expected, but when these landed without permission and hoisted the Argentinian flag, the matter assumed a different complexion. Graphic accounts of the events following this, leading to an armed attack on King Edward Point by Argentinian forces on 3 April 1982, and its retaking by the British just over three weeks later, have been given by Robert Headland, who was in charge of the BAS party which took refuge in the Grytviken church, and by the military and naval historian, Roger Perkins.[88] The signal from the officer accepting the Argentine surrender – 'Be pleased to inform Her Majesty that the White Ensign flies alongside the Union Flag in Grytviken, South Georgia. God save the Queen' – comfortingly reasserted old-time values, but things could not be the same for the Fids again. Those on South Georgia had provided valuable information and intelligence and BAS experience had been useful in the Falklands conflict. This they could be proud of, but on the other hand the international camaradarie of Antarctic science had been compromised. The scientists at Grytviken had been removed as prisoners with only twenty minutes to collect personal belongings and scientific records. Not only were research programmes violently disrupted, but the station was looted and material and data disappeared. Because it has been necessary to maintain a British military presence at King Edward Point, BAS has not been able to reoccupy it and only at Bird Island has the research programme continued without interruption. However, realizing the necessity of an increased British presence in the Antarctic, the government has augmented the grants available to BAS generally.

The future of South Georgia remains obscure. An economic report made in 1982 by Lord Shackleton, son of the explorer, identified krill, fish and squid as possible resources for exploitation.[89] Already, unregulated fishing around South Georgia has depleted stock and the establishment of a 320-kilometre (200-mile) fishing zone around the island would permit conservation and, to judge by the example of the Falkland Islands, bring in substantial revenues from licences. Now that seals are thriving again, humane and scientifically controlled culling of these is possible and might well be justifiable on ecological grounds. Hydrocarbon and other mineral resources do not seem at present to be worth considering but if developments were to happen further south, South Georgia, with its magnificent natural harbours, would provide a splendid base for operations.

Many things make South Georgia a potential tourist attraction – the scenery is wonderfully beautiful, wildlife is abundant and entertaining, and the historical associations are many – but the highly unpredictable weather and the unstable terrain, resulting from rapid transition between freeze and thaw, make the island even more dangerous perhaps than the Antarctic continent itself. Fatalities from avalanches and the 'williwaws', sudden squalls which swoop down from the mountains and transform flat calm to inferno in a few minutes, have happened in the past. Duncan Carse, who had led several expeditions to South Georgia, made the experiment in 1961 of living alone near Undine South Harbour on the south-west coast and had his hut washed away by a surge wave shortly after he had established himself. Fortunately he managed to salvage sufficient essentials to survive for nearly four months until he was able to contact a passing ship. In 1975, a tremendous fall of rock from near the summit of the 1800-metre (5900-foot) Paulsen Peak, just behind Grytviken, deposited an estimated 210,000 cubic metres (275,000 cubic yards) of debris on the glacier below, mercifully when no glaciologists were working on it, and released an enormous cloud of dust. During the 1982 operations an 'insertion' of military personnel on the Fortuna Glacier, made against BAS advice in full confidence that the SAS could cope with anything, went badly astray with the loss of two helicopters but, fortunately, no lives. As with the rest of the Antarctic, the most satisfactory future for South Georgia would be to leave it undisturbed as a patch of wilderness in an otherwise increasingly man-handled world.

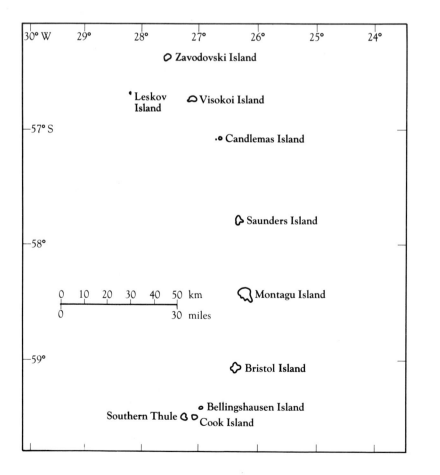

The South Sandwich
Islands

Chapter Six

The Antarctic
Archipelagos

S OME OF THE peri-Antarctic islands – Prince Edward, Crozet, Kerguelen, Macquarie – lie, like South Georgia, near to the Convergence, and like it have slightly more varied floras and faunas than
those further south. Some of the more southerly islands – Balleny, Scott,
Peter I, Bouvet, Heard – are isolated, to a greater or lesser extent inaccessible, and much less supportive of wildlife. Others, grouped in the archipelagos of the South Sandwiches, South Orkneys and South Shetlands, are
of more interest to the naturalist and historian. These island groups,
together with South Georgia, are the higher peaks of a submarine ridge, the
Scotia Ridge, which forms a huge eastward extending loop linking the
Andes of South America and the mountain chain of the Peninsula.

The South Sandwich Islands – named after the First Lord of the Admiralty who sent James Cook into Antarctic waters – lie in a chain across the
stream of ice projected up from the Weddell Sea. They are about as far from
any other land as they could be and to their loneliness is added weirdness
because, although they have permanent ice, they are also volcanic. The
South Sandwich Islands were discovered by Captain Cook, who called one
of them Southern Thule 'because it is the most southern land that has ever
yet been discovered'. They were visited some forty-five years later by Captain Bellingshausen who discovered and named the most northerly members of the group, one of them, Zavodovski, having an active volcano.
Lieutenant-Commander Ivan Zavodovski landed and ascended half-way
up his volcano, where he found the ground warm, but was driven back by
what he described as 'a particularly bad smell from the great quantity of

guano from the penguins'. Zavodovski Island is reported as having as many as 14 million penguins on it, and it may well be that their effluvium obliterated any fumes that the volcano produced. Candlemas Island, named by Cook, is also volcanic and its uncanny feel is evident in the place-names given by the British Antarctic Survey team which surveyed it in 1964 – Lucifer Hill, Breakbones Plateau, Kraken Cove, Gorgon Pool, Chimaera Flats, Sarcophagus Point. Good use has been made of this island by Ian Cameron as a setting for his not absolutely implausible story of marine biology, romance and the supernatural, *The White Ship*.[90] The only people actually to have lived on these inhospitable islands for any length of time have been 'technicians' at a clandestine station established on Southern Thule by Argentina in 1976. No doubt those in residence at the time were greatly relieved to be removed by HMS *Endurance* in a cleaning-up operation after the Falklands conflict.[91]

The volcanic activity on the South Sandwiches is striking but a not less remarkable feature is only evident on a map. Searching for them in an atlas, the tiny dots of the islands seem lost besides a tremendous crescent-shaped trench, in which the sea bottom falls precipitously from 1000 to over 7000 metres (3800 to 23,000 feet), outlining the arc of the Scotia Ridge to the west. The volcanic activity and this trench are both manifestations of events which, quite literally, have shaped the world we live in.

American whaling station, Kerguelen. (Wild, *At Anchor*, 1878: courtesy of the Scott Polar Research Institute)

In 1912 a German meteorologist and explorer, Alfred Wegener, crystallized an idea, which had been vaguely perceived before, when he pointed out that the continents fit together like the pieces of a jigsaw puzzle, not only as regards their outlines but in the patterns of geological formation and animal and plant distributions which they bear. He proposed that the continents once formed a single land mass, which he called Pangaea, and that it split up, with the bits, the present continents, drifting apart in the course of geological time. It is said, plausibly but without any written evidence, that this idea came to him when he saw an ice-floc splitting up in the Arctic. His hypothesis was ridiculed – there is, alas, in some scientists an arrogant faith in their theoretical deductions which blinds them to facts – because no convincing mechanisms for moving continents around could be suggested. However, by the 1960s, further evidence had come along which geophysicists could not ignore and Wegener's theory of continental drift has not only been accepted but has revolutionized thought in the earth sciences. The continents are seen as being mounted on tectonic plates which are carried on the underlying oceanic crust and pushed apart by convection currents in the semi-fluid mantle below. The heat which produces the convection currents, and therefore the energy for shifting the continents, is provided by radioactivity in the earth's core.

Antarctica – which, together with central and southern Africa, peninsular India, Australia and South America, formed at one time a supercontinent called Gondwanaland – seems always to have been in the vicinity of the South Pole. South America was the last continent to separate from Antarctica and the opening of the Drake Passage was one of the earth's major events. It allowed the establishment of the circumpolar current and this led to the climatic isolation of the Antarctic continent, that in turn to the formation of the ice-cap and that to the present pattern of world climate. The loop of the Scotia Ridge suggests that some sideways-acting force broke the land bridge between Antarctica and South America, but things were evidently much more complicated than that. The geological development of the area is still not fully understood but, to get back to the South Sandwich Islands, they stand at the eastern end of a small tectonic plate, the Sandwich Plate, which is sandwiched (and since we have got involved with it, Cook's Sandwich also gave his name to the portable meal) between two convectional spreading centres. At the eastern edge the ocean floor is being pushed beneath the tectonic plate ('subduction' is the technical term) and the trench has formed where it goes under. The buried oceanic crust heats up and produces the lavas and steam which ascend to give rise to volcanoes and thermal springs.[92]

After visiting the South Sandwiches, Cook did not probe much further south. He believed that there was land to the south. Captain Cook was then two and a half years out from home and:

> Thick fogs, Snow storms, Intense Cold and every other thing that can render Navigation dangerous one has to encounter and these difficulties are greatly heightned by the enexpressable horrid aspect of the Country... After such an explanation as this the reader must not expect to find me much farther to the South. It is however not for want of inclination but other reasons. It would have been rashness in me to have risked all which had been done in the Voyage, in finding out and exploaring a Coast which when done would have answered no end whatever, or have been the least use either to Navigation or Geography or indeed to any other Science.[93]

There was land to the south but it was 1600 kilometres (1000 miles) away. Rather nearer, 800 kilometres (500 miles) to the west-south-west was another group of islands which remained undiscovered for another forty-six years. These, the South Orkney Islands, again are part of the Scotia Ridge, but no subduction is occurring in their vicinity and they are not volcanic.

The South Orkneys were discovered in 1821 by a British sealer, George Powell, captain of the sloop *Dove*, in company with the American Nathaniel Palmer, captaining the sloop *James Monroe*. By that time very few seals were left on the South Shetlands and, when the two ships met at Elephant Island, Powell's suggestion that they should join forces to explore to the north-east was readily accepted by Palmer. They soon encountered foul weather, then ice, but steering south-east to avoid this, what appeared to be land was

The South Orkney Islands

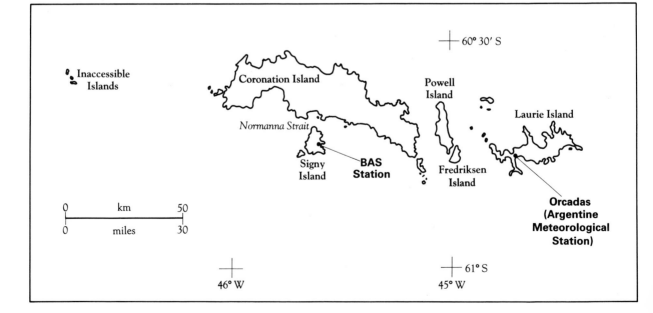

Ice-floes, evening (oil)

sighted. The *James Monroe* was some 6 kilometres (4 miles) astern of the *Dove* and, as Powell recorded: 'Captain Palmer doubted whether it was land or ice; but, at all events, he said he would follow me.' It was land and Powell took possession of it, naming it Coronation Isle with the thought that it was the first land discovered since the coronation of King George IV. There were no seals to be found and Palmer seems to have accepted the appropriation by the British of this worthless discovery without demur. Navigation around the islands is hazardous: they lie close to the track of the circumpolar depressions, for most of the year they are surrounded by ice and more often than not they are enveloped in fog. The French expedition under d'Urville visited the South Orkneys briefly in 1838 but otherwise they seem to have been left for the most part in obscurity until, in 1903–4, the Scottish National Antarctic Expedition under Dr W. S. Bruce established a meteorological station on one of the group, Laurie Island, and carried out surveys and scientific work. As has already been mentioned, this station has been run by Argentina ever since Bruce left it.[94]

Besides Coronation and Laurie Islands, the other large member of the group is Powell Island. All three of them are permanently snow- and ice-covered. One of the smaller islands, Signy Island, which is only about 8 kilometres (5 miles) in length, has much of its rock exposed in a good summer and has on it the British Antarctic Survey's chief biological station. Once it was a base for whaling – a Norwegian whaler named the island after his wife – and its beaches are littered with the bones of whales. Waterpipe

Landing from the *Astrolabe* and *Zelée* on Weddell Island, South Orkney group, 20 February 1838. Lithograph after L. le Breton. (d'Urville, *Atlas Pittoresque*, 1841–5, vol. 1, plate 26: courtesy of the Scott Polar Research Institute)

Beach, where the whalers used to water their vessels from a pipeline leading down from Pumphouse Lake, had until recently a weather-worn notice bearing the words 'British Crown Property'. On a point near Factory Cove, befouled by sea elephants, is a row of five graves marked by simple wooden crosses, one labelled minimally 'Unknown Whaler'. A dismal place to leave one's bones, perhaps, but on the rare clear evening, when the setting sun suffuses with rose the snow-clad peaks of Coronation Island over on the other side of Normanna Strait, one knows that these whalers rest in peace.

There is a surprising amount of greenery on Signy Island. The exposed rocks are lichen-covered and there are large patches of moss, some of which top peat banks which radiocarbon dating has shown as having been laid down some 2000 years ago. The only two indigenous flowering plants of the Antarctic, a grass, *Deschampsia antarctica*, and *Colobanthus quitenis*, a relative of the garden pink, are also to be found in sheltered, north-facing spots. Like the mosses, these plants form cushions which are effective miniature greenhouses, getting up to as much as 20°C (68°F) in the sun. It is in these warm intervals that the plants manage to achieve their growth; all the rest of the time it is a matter of endurance. Besides cold and snow cover for three-quarters of the year, the plants have to contend with high winds, which cause desiccation, and frequent alternation of freezing and thawing, which produces soil heaving. This heaving sorts out stones and silt to form polygons on the flat and stripes on hillsides.

The details of how any plants – algae, lichens, mosses or flowering plants – survive under such adverse conditions are of great interest to BAS ecologists. Information about the microclimates of different patches of vegetation on Signy Island is collected from instruments left permanently in position

Graves of sealers, Betsy Cove, Kerguelen. (Wild, *At Anchor*, 1878: courtesy of the Scott Polar Research Institute)

Ice cliff, Weddell Sea (oil)

and recorded on electronic data-loggers. From these records the crucial episodes which determine the survival or otherwise of particular species can be worked out. Grazing by large animals is not a hazard, although damage by trampling may perhaps take a hundred years to repair, and the mosses seem not to be eaten by anything. Algae, other microbes, and dead organic matter are fed on by numerous small mites and springtails. Most of the plant production, however, is slowly broken down by bacteria and fungi followed mechanical disruption by freeze-thaw cycles.[92] Often snow on Signy becomes coloured with patches of delicate pink or yellow, brilliant scarlet or green and since these appear almost overnight it seems that something is able to grow rapidly even on this unpromising substrate. Examination under the microscope shows the organisms to be algae – one is *Chlamydomonas nivalis*, a green unicellular form of which other species are found in farmyard ponds, which exists in snow mainly as red-coloured spores. They do not actually grow very quickly but, since they are collected at the snow surface as it disappears by melting or sublimation, the patches can appear suddenly in a period of thaw.

Signy has numerous small lakes, some, which get the drainage from elephant seal wallows, supporting a rich soup of algal growth, others, surrounded by snow field or glacial moraine, devoid of any sort of life to the eye of the non-expert. Since they are sealed off by being frozen for most of the year and contain no animal life larger than a freshwater shrimp, they are different from temperate freshwaters and one or two of them, having been studied in detail for many years, are now classic examples of Antarctic lakes.[92] The uninformed may be excused for overlooking their interest; in shallow water a drab ochreous or olive-green algal felt covering the stones is all that can be seen and the luxuriant growth of aquatic moss which, surprisingly, is to be found in some of them, is out of sight except for the scuba diver. The non-living contents may seem more interesting as sometimes the ice forms in vertical prisms, so-called 'candle ice', which, when the lake begins to thaw, fall apart and look like the wreck of a chandelier floating on the water.

Among the larger animals around the shores of Signy there are elephant and fur seals, about which something has already been said, and adelie and chinstrap penguins. The two penguin species, which are rather similar except that the one has a black strap under its chin, occupy overlapping sites but on the whole keep segregated. The adelie extends further south than does the chinstrap, however. Their colonies are noisome with the reddish sludge of their excrement underfoot and a really high-powered stench arising from it. Passage through a colony brings a new incident with every step. Most birds take exception to an outsized interloper and go for his accessible parts with blows from hard and muscular flippers and powerful jabs from sharp beaks. However, another penguin may decide that it is her spouse who is at the bottom of all the trouble and, assailing him, starts a general fight. An attacking penguin may quite suddenly forget what it is he is supposed to be doing and relapse into an introspective haze. Or another may conclude that here at last in this giant penguin he has found the perfect mate and lay a love-offering of a pebble at one's feet.

Apart from such minor infidelities, it seems that penguins are faithful to one mate for life. Courtship involves the birds going into 'ecstasy', standing facing each other, rocking from side to side, with bills raised high and squawking heavenwards. The nest is rudimentary in the extreme but the few pebbles which serve to raise the bird slightly above the general unpleasantness are precious symbols, much sought after and to be stolen if possible. L. C. Bernacchi described the thieving that went on in the Cape Adare colony as follows:

> The thief slowly approaches the one he wishes to rob with a most creditable air of nonchalance and disinterestedness, and if, on getting closer, the other looks at him suspiciously, he will immediately gaze round almost child-like and bland, and appear to be admiring the scenery. The assumption of innocence is perfect; but no sooner does the other look in a different direction, then he will dart down on one of the pebbles of its nest and scamper away with it in his beak.[95]

Two eggs are laid per nest and the parents take turns in incubating them, and, later on, in feeding the chicks. The rearing of the chicks is timed to coincide with the period of maximum abundance of krill. As with the other penguins, the young are fed with food regurgitated from the parent's crop. The young chicks are pretty but the older ones are horrors – their down becomes matted with filth and their figures bulge downwards like plastic bags filled with water. After about four weeks they congregate in crèches of as many as a hundred under the guard of a few older birds. This serves as a protection against the skuas, which attack stragglers. After moulting, the juveniles go off to fend for themselves in February.

In the water their principal foe is the leopard seal. There is an irresistible temptation to interpret penguin behaviour in human terms, but the often-told story of penguins at the ice-edge jostling each other until one falls in, whereupon the others peer over the edge to see whether a leopard seal gets him, appears to be correct. Penguins fly rather than swim under water; their bodies are beautifully streamlined and their cruising speed is around 13 knots, with twice this attainable in short bursts. When travelling long distances they porpoise in and out of the water. To land on rocks or ice standing above the water, they accelerate upwards and shoot out of the water nearly vertically. When a penguin mistakes a boat for a rock, the bird and the boatman get equal shocks. On land, penguins can plod along at about 3 kilometers (2 miles) per hour but, by going down on their fronts and tobog-ganing, they can outpace a sprinting man.[96]

The skua just mentioned is disliked by the Fids, who call it the brown bomber, almost as much as it is by penguins. Paranoia about skuas is one of the themes in G. Billing's novel *Forbush and the Penguins*.[97] It is a large, handsome, gull-like bird with strong territorial instincts, which it shows by making terrifying and repeated swoops at a human intruder, sometimes so close as to strike his head with a wing. It also has magpie instincts and will make off with thermometers or lens caps left lying around, or root up care-fully arranged experimental material from moss swards. They often nest near penguin colonies and each pair has its own area which is defended from other skuas and scavenged for abandoned eggs and sickly or dead chicks. Sometimes a pair will co-operate by one distracting a penguin while the other takes its egg, or by jointly attacking a chick. They also catch fish and krill for themselves or pirate these from other birds.[96] Skuas around bases take scraps and two pairs have divided the Signy station between them with a scrupu-lously observed boundary running down the middle of the jetty. Skuas occasionally appear far inland on the continental ice-cap where there cannot possibly be any food for them; Scott's party had a visit from one at 87°20′S on their march across the plateau towards the Pole. More recently, the 90° South expedition led by Monica Kristensen, following in Amundsen's tracks, encountered three plump skuas at 86°S.

Marine biology at Signy depends very much on a team of divers for studies of the plants and animals of inshore waters. The shores of Signy look barren but, once one gets down below the scour of drifting ice, there are dense beds of seaweed, huge sponges and a wealth of bizarre kinds of animals.

Leaving the South Orkneys and following the Scotia Ridge to the east-south-east brings one to the South Shetland Islands. As related in Chapter Two, these were discovered around 1820 and quickly became the scene of frantic sealing. Now they are again one of the busiest parts of the Antarctic. The largest of the group, King George Island (fortuitously it has perched on a hillside a pinnacle of rock which looks like a crowned figure seated on a throne), has no less than eight research stations on it and, as already noted, is regularly visited by tourist planes and ships. The most recently established bases are the People's Republic of China's Great Wall station and South Korea's King Sejong station. The Soviet Bellingshausen station and the Chilean Teniente Rodolfo Marsh (formerly Presidente Frei) station represent similar political extremes and are sited within a few hundred yards of each other. They have co-existed for many years and, as far as the casual visitor can tell, are on amicable terms. The two bases co-operate in meteorological observations, play each other at football, and the Chileans supply the Soviets with pin-ups. For a scientist visiting them off a research vessel memories of these two stations tend to be hazy, since each regards it as a point of honour to outdo the other in hospitality.

Elephant Island is one of the least hospitable of the South Shetland Islands. It was on this island that Shackleton and his men landed after their long drift on the ice of the Weddell Sea and perilous boat journey after the ice broke up:

> It was the first landing ever made on Elephant Island, and I thought the honour should belong to Blackborrow, the youngest member of the Expedition, but I had forgotten that his frost-bitten feet would prevent him from appreciating the honour thrust upon him.
>
> We landed the cook with his blubber-stove, a supply of fuel, and some packets of dried milk, and also several of the men. Then the rest of us pulled out again to pilot the other boats through the channel, and within a few minutes the three boats were aground.
>
> When I landed for the second time a curious spectacle met my eyes. Some of the men were reeling about the beach as if they were intoxicated.

The South Shetland Islands

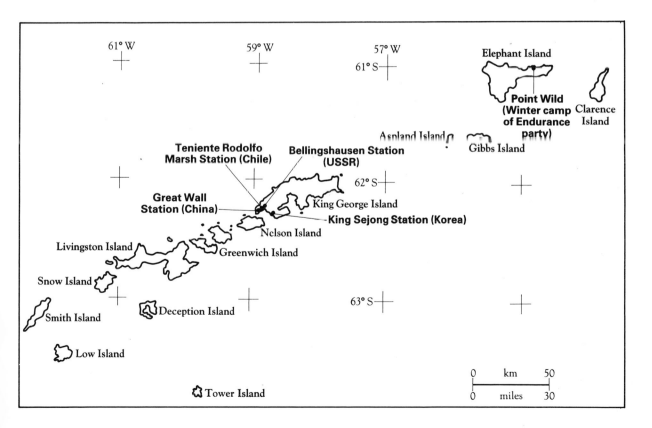

147

They were laughing uproariously, picking up stones and letting handfuls of pebbles trickle between their fingers, like misers gloating over hoarded gold.[98]

The joy of being on solid ground was soon to give way to extreme misery again. The first task was to get the *James Caird* into as good a shape as possible for the voyage to South Georgia which Shackleton saw as the only way of obtaining rescue. She was decked in with plywood and canvas over a framework made of sledge runners, her keel was reinforced with the mast from another boat and the artist Marston's oil paints were commandeered for caulking. After Shackleton and his five companions had sailed, the remaining twenty-two men had to face a long period of waiting and uncertainty under abysmal conditions. Their shelter consisted of the two remaining boats, upturned, their only source of heat was blubber, which produced quantities of acrid smoke and soot, and except for a few odd cases of 'palate ticklers' brought from the ship, their food was what the shore would yield. They were continually on the verge of starvation, but mercifully the odd penguin or seal always turned up before things became too serious. The weather was evil. Gangrene had destroyed the toes of Blackborrow's left foot

Elephant Island, South Shetland group. Lithograph after E. Goupil. (d'Urville, *Atlas Pittoresque*, 1841–5, vol 1, plate 27: courtesy of the Scott Polar Research Institute)

and they had to be amputated, which was done successfully in spite of the utterly primitive and filthy conditions.

Conservative estimates were that a rescue ship might arrive by the beginning of June, six weeks after the sailing of the *James Caird*. This date came and went and, although Frank Wild kept morale wonderfully high all things considered, each man thought privately that they were there at least for the winter and probably for ever. The arrival of Shackleton in the Chilean schooner *Yelcho* on 30 August, the time when the winter ice-cover usually reaches its maximum, was therefore high drama. Not surprisingly, accounts of this event differ in detail, but all agree that the Elephant Island party was just about to start its mid-day meal. Marston, who had gone to the lookout bluff to make some sketches, was late and when he was heard running towards the hut this was no more than expected. Short of breath and struggling with emotion his question: 'Hadn't we better send up some smoke signals?' came out uncertainly. For a few moments there was uncomprehending silence then there was a wild rush in which the precious boiled seal's backbone went underfoot and the hut was wrecked. One of his comrades had thought for Blackborrow, went back, and carried him to a place where he could see the ship headed towards them. The last tin of biscuits was broken open and offered around without any one counting but mostly the men were too excited even for this unheard-of indulgence. Hurley, ever the photographer, expended his last three exposures on the scene as a boat with Shackleton in it approached the shore. Once again Providence had given Shackleton a small window, with favourable weather and ice conditions, through which he had come triumphantly to save the entire company he had started out with.[41]

A similar enforced sojourn on a South Shetland island – shorter in duration but scarcely less awful for the men concerned, especially since they had not been hardened by six month's exposure on ice and in open boats beforehand – has happened since. A party of six men from *Discovery II* was left with the launch *Rapid* to carry out a survey of a section of the coast of King George Island in January 1937. The inshore waters of this archipelago, which present a maze of shallow channels, reefs and submerged rocks, could not be surveyed from a large ship. The *Rapid* was a sturdy craft but her engine, running on crude oil, needed coaxing at the best of times and failed completely soon after the party had been left while the *Discovery II* did work elsewhere. The weather became foul and the men thought it safer to leave the anchored boat, by now leaking badly through the buffeting she had received, for the comparative safety of the shore. They were right to do so because the *Rapid* foundered shortly after. Living under the shelter of their upturned pram, with only two soaking two-man sleeping bags between them, like Shackleton's men they had to resort to eating penguin and seal and burning their blubber for heat. When the *Discovery II* returned to the rendezvous and found it deserted, an alarm was sent out and HMS *Ajax*, cruising Falkland waters, and the *Penola*, on her way down to the British Graham Land Expedition's base on the Peninsula, joined in the search. The party was found twelve days after it had been left to do its survey, to the frustration of the evil spirit which F. D. Ommanney,[99] who wrote a first-hand account of the miseries it inflicted, felt must dwell in those parts. Portable radios are now the means of keeping the spirit frustrated.

Elephant Island was occasionally landed on but not explored until sixty years after Shackleton's men left it. Then British Joint Services expeditions visited it in 1970–1 and 1976–7. On the second expedition, with Commander Chris Furse as its leader, surveys of Elephant Island and its neighbour Clarence Island were made over a period of twelve weeks. Two parties of eight men were landed by helicopter from HMS *Endurance*, but canoes were used for transport around the islands. In view of what has already been said about conditions around these islands this choice of craft may seem astonishing. The weather made no concessions and out of the ten canoes taken only three survived but no lives were lost. There were first ascents of various peaks including Mount Irving, 1924 metres (6312 feet) high, on Clarence Island and work was done on the geology, botany and zoology of the islands. On the 1971 expedition the sites occupied by Shackleton and his men were visited but no traces of them could be found.[100]

The oddest island in the South Shetland group, Deception Island, is not as frequented now as it used to be. This is because, lying as it does at the corner of a small tectonic plate with a subduction zone just to the north, it is volcanic and not to be trusted. The island itself is the rim of a volcano, the crater of which has been flooded by the sea. A narrow gap in the rim, Neptune's Bellows, leads to the basin of Port Foster, about 8 kilometres (5 miles) across and as perfect a harbour as one could hope to find in these stormy seas. Its shores have brick-red rocks, beaches of black volcanic ash and, if one feels inclined that way, one can take a bath in a hot spring surrounded by snow and interested penguins. For a long time these hot springs were the only manifestations of volcanic activity.

After its discovery, probably by Nathaniel Palmer in 1820, Deception was frequently used as a convenient harbour. Captain Henry Foster in HMS *Chanticleer* was there in 1829 for the 'peculiar object' of timing the swinging of a pendulum.[101] This is not quite so eccentric an object as it may appear, because such measurements can be used to calculate the shape of the earth, information about which was at that time becoming necessary for accurate mapping. The name Pendulum Cove on the map of Deception Island is a reminder of that visit. Foster left a self-registering thermometer on the island, which was sought, but not found, when the *Sea Gull* of the

Wilkes expedition put in there in 1839. However, the *Sea Gull* left a note about it in a bottle and this led to its discovery by the sealer James Smyley in 1842, when it read − 20.5°C (− 5°F). Later on, Deception became a flourishing whaling depot, with catches equalling those of South Georgia.

After the Second World War, Argentine, British and Chilean scientific bases were established on the island. In 1967 Deception Island erupted. The Fids, after making sure of their photographs of the events taking place, succouring the Chileans, whose base was wrecked, and collecting a few belongings – in that order – were evacuated by a helicopter from the Argentinian vessel *Bahia Aguirre*. When this phase of activity subsided a new island, 60 metres (200 feet) high and nearly a kilometre (half a mile) in length, had appeared in Port Foster. All seemed quiet again and the British base was reoccupied but a second eruption a year later, which wrecked many huts and swept the whalers' graveyard into the sea, decided the Survey to abandon the island as a permanent base.

The mountains of the Antarctic Peninsula can just be seen from Deception Island on its rare clear days and it was on forays from the South Shetlands that this part of the Antarctic continent was discovered and first explored.

The rescue from Elephant Island, 30 August 1916; photo Frank Hurley. (Courtesy of the Scott Polar Research Institute)

151

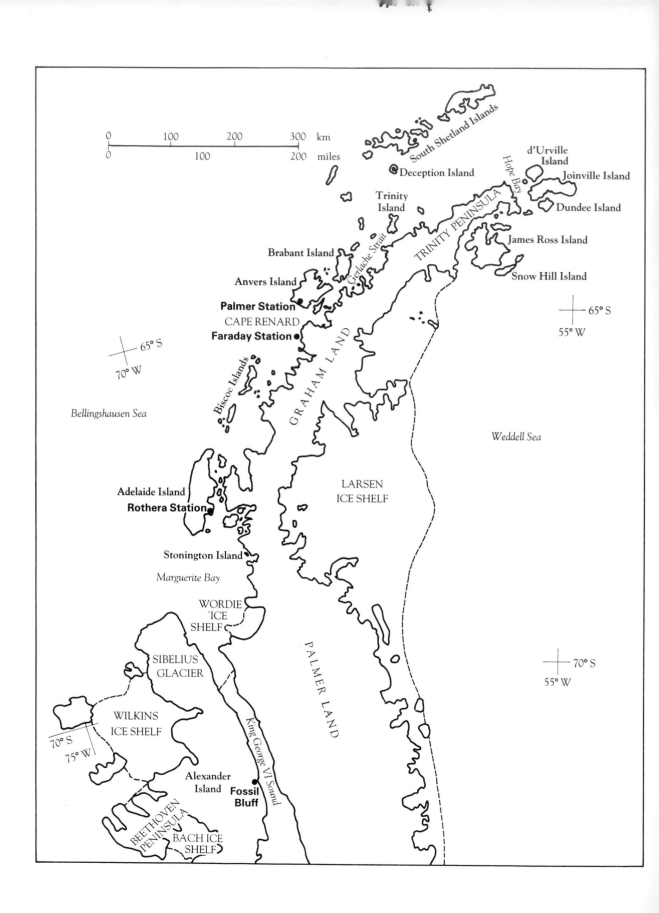

Chapter Seven

The Antarctic Peninsula

THE PANHANDLE of the continent is best called the Antarctic Peninsula; this avoids upsetting British insularity, which would have it called Graham Land after a highly unpopular First Lord of the Admiralty, American partiality, which named it the Palmer Peninsula after the second man to sight it, and Argentine and Chilean desires, which have it as Tierra San Martin and Tierra O'Higgins respectively, after national heroes. Graham Land and Palmer Land are retained, the former for the north and the latter for the south regions of the Peninsula.

The Peninsula does not have the stupendous panoramas of the Ross Sea area but its scenery is of a more intimate, varied kind and there is general agreement that it is the most beautiful that the beautiful continent of Antarctica has to offer. This mainly depends on the precipitous character of the land, with its abundance of rock faces too near the vertical to hold snow. The monolith of Cape Renard rises sheer out of the sea to a height of 747 metres (2450 feet). Lemaire Channel is a narrow cutting, its sides perpendicular and draped with glaciers, between Booth Island and Cape Cloos. Unless it is blocked by an iceberg, it gives a safe, sheltered and awe-inspiring passage to ships, and perhaps more film is expended in it than anywhere else on the Peninsula. At sunrise and sunset mountains and snow-fields are suffused with washes of rose, salmon-pink and gold, which are reflected in the sea and set off by dark rock and the blue of snow in the shadows.

Bearing in mind that the sea bottom is likely to be as rugged as what is seen above water, *The Antarctic Pilot* does well to remark that in these parts

The Antarctic Peninsula

153

'an efficient and keen lookout is absolutely essential for safe navigation'. Even this cannot always prevent accidents. David Smith was aboard the *Bransfield* when she ran on to an uncharted rock off the southern tip of Adelaide Island in Marguerite Bay in March 1980:

> The weather was absolutely brilliant. We were in radio contact with Rothera base – now only about an hour away, and everything was going fine. I was on the port side of the bridge, making a watercolour of the wind ahead driving the water-lily ice in streaks towards us; everyone was in a jolly mood. Suddenly there was a most violent shudder and grinding noise. I was thrown hard forward against my drawing board, which broke in two, giving from the force of the impact. Then there was another rending, scraping crash and the ship reeled and came to a stand-still, listing to starboard. Something serious had happened. Somehow I felt superfluous. I caught sight of the Radio Officer's face as he dashed to the bridge. He looked ashen-grey. Later he told me that he thought an explosion had taken place in the engine room. Captain Cole looked very calm. Immediately he had the mate Graham Phippen and the crew inspecting the ship. They took soundings all round her, and also through the small hatches on deck leading to the tanks. Some slicks of oil were on the surface of the water . . . *Bransfield* had sailed down this route many times and the echo-sounding chart showed adequate clearance of water underneath the vessel. There must have been one particular jagged needle-like rock, and the ship was on it before the echo-sounder showed anything. RRS *Bransfield* is a very strongly built ship with a double hull, and it was found that although several outer plates had been pierced, there was no trace of water through the inner casings. Having found the depth of water on the port and starboard sides, the water tanks on the port side were pumped empty and those on the starboard side filled. The ship now had an intentional list to starboard, so that the tilt raising our port side, plus the fact that the tide had eighteen inches to make, our engines running astern plus careful rudder manoeuvring, made it possible to ease her off the rocks . . . After four hours we were on our way to Rothera base where we arrived an hour later. I thought the whole operation was a magnificent example of cool, calm, disciplined seamanship.
>
> (Diary of David Smith)

More recently, in January 1989, the Argentine supply vessel *Bahia Paraiso* was not so fortunate 400 kilometres (250 miles) to the north of this. She sank; all 300 passengers were rescued but there was an oil spill which put thousands of nesting penguins at risk.

The scenery of the Peninsula derives, of course, from the geology. Antarctica is a difficult place for the traditional geologist because most of its rock is

Low sun and icebergs (water-colour)

under thousands of feet of ice and much of the 1 per cent of the land surface which is exposed is not easy to get at. In this case, one may ask, why bother? Antarctica's rocks cannot be so very different from those which can be more conveniently studied elsewhere.

The answer, already touched on in the previous chapter and compelling to anyone who wants to understand how our planet came to be as it is, is that Antarctica lay at the heart of the supercontinent, Gondwanaland, of which South America, Africa, India and Australia were other pieces now forced apart by sea-floor spreading from lines of weakness. Antarctica fits neatly into the jigsaw of these other bits and the geology around its edges mostly matches up with that of the edges of the other continents with which it is supposed to have once been contiguous. Whereas the other fragments of Gondwanaland have moved northward in the 180 to 200 million years which have elapsed since the breakup occurred, Antarctica has moved little, only drifting slowly southwards to its present position around the South Pole.

The fly in the ointment of this majestic concept is the Antarctic Peninsula. Whereas Greater or East Antarctica consists largely of an intact, stable shield of ancient Precambrian rock, the Peninsula, which is part of Lesser or West Antarctica, is built of younger rocks which do not fit into the Gondwana pattern. Much of its rocks are sedimentary, of Jurassic to Cretaceous age – 175 to 65 million years – with extensive intrusions of igneous rocks as evidence of volcanic activity up to about 10 million years ago. The sedimentary rocks have yielded plant and animal fossils, some new to science and others showing affinities with South American and Asian forms. It is clear that at one time the climate of the Peninsula must have been much more genial than it is at present. How the complex structures of the Peninsula and the Scotia Ridge are to be interpreted is still not at all clear. However, it seems that, after the breakup of the supercontinent, which took place from late Jurassic times (that is, some 150 million years ago) until comparatively recently, the Peninsula area was a subduction zone where the crust of the Pacific Ocean floor was being pushed below the edge of a plate. This lifted up the sedimentary rocks of the plate and caused volcanic activity and intrusions of igneous rocks, the result being the mountainous spine of the Peninsula. The situation, in fact, was very much like the present one along the west coast of South America.[102]

A hard-headed justification for geology in the Peninsula region might be that valuable minerals are to be found there (see page 202). Certainly geological resemblances to the Andes, stretches of which contain some of the richest metal-producing areas in the world, suggest this. However, such land that is accessible to prospecting in the Peninsula has not shown any valuable deposits. Copper, iron, molybdenum, lead, zinc and silver have been found, but a deposit would have to be very valuable to make it worth while exploiting in this part of the world. There is no definite evidence of oil as yet in Antarctica and, if there were, drilling for it would be far more expensive even than it is in Alaska, where the oil fields are only just economically viable.

Ice does not totally prevent geological survey, even if it does come between the geologist's hammer and the rocks. Minute variations in the earth's gravitational and magnetic fields show up small variations in the specific gravity and magnetic content of rocks beneath ice can yield information about structures, discontinuities and rock compositions. Since magnetometers can be operated from aircraft, information can be obtained from terrain inaccessible to ground parties.

Sailing down the west side of the Peninsula, the first two large islands to be met with are Brabant and Anvers. The Belgian flavour in the names hereabouts derives from the *Belgica* expedition under de Gerlache in 1898–9, the first scientific expedition to explore the Peninsula.[29] Brabant Island, which had hitherto experienced only five brief landings since its discovery, was thoroughly explored in 1983–4 by another Joint Services expedition under Commander Chris Furse. The team included Francois de Gerlache de Gomery, grandson of the man who discovered Brabant Island. For a year they lived in tents and snow-holes, being the first expedition to pass an Antarctic winter without a base hut, and they circumnavigated the island by kayak.[103]

Anvers Island was probably discovered by John Biscoe in 1832, but he thought the land to which he rowed ashore and took possession of in the name of His Majesty King William IV was part of the mainland. In 1954–5 a FIDS base was established on the island, below the towering massif of Mount Français (2672 metres – 8766 feet), where there was an almost land-locked harbour. This was closed after two years of survey and geological investigation, but later in 1965 an adjacent site was used for the US Palmer Station. Its two main blue and white buildings now stand on a rocky promontory on the edge of the ice piedmont and sheltered from the worst of the sea by numerous islands. There is an abundance of life – seals, penguins, patches of green moss on the islands, and all sorts of sea creatures in the inshore waters below the reach of the ice – and Palmer is a focus for biological studies. The station is comfortable, spacious and warm, linked by radio with civilization and yet in intimate contact with the icy world outside. There is usually some interesting ice-formation or spectacular cloud formation to be seen from the windows of its common room and often there is a thunderous rumbling from the snout of the nearby glacier as a mass of ice the size of an office-block collapses into the sea.

Palmer Station's research vessel was until recently the *Hero*, named after

Caved iceberg (oil)

Nathaniel Palmer's sloop. She was built in 1968 especially for Antarctic work – 38 metres (125 feet) long, wooden with steel-sheathed bows and round-bottomed to avoid being gripped by ice. To reduce the rolling inseparable from a round bottom she was ketch-rigged to carry sail, although powered with a 760 horse-power motor. She was a distinctive sight in southern waters with her green hull and red sails. She demoralized a succession of skippers but did what was wanted of her well and the final departure from Antarctic waters in 1984 of 'that goddamn green dragon', because of incipient dry rot in her oak timbers, was a matter of sadness.[104] *Hero* was too small to carry much cargo and for many years supplies for Palmer have been brought in by the BAS vessel *Bransfield*.

The region just south of Anvers Island is particularly associated with the Frenchman Jean-Baptiste Charcot, who led two expeditions to the Peninsula, one in the *Français* in 1903–5 and the second in the *Pourquoi-Pas?* in 1908–10. He left a scattering of French names along the Peninsula and on the summit of Petermann Island, at which *Pourquoi-Pas?* wintered, a plaque listing the members of his expedition. Scott described him as 'the gentleman of the Pole', because he refrained from exploring in the Ross Sea area which Scott had earmarked as his own. He was certainly an attractive character and greatly concerned for the morale of his men. There was an ample supply of French and other wines aboard the *Pourquoi-Pas?*, but he kept the consumption of these under control and was equally careful with mental stimulants. Mentioning that the ship's library contained about 1500 volumes, he said:

> The crew has the right of dipping into these to a great extent, but I have thought it best to strike off the catalogue for their use a whole series of volumes that seemed to me harmful, or at least useless, to most of these good fellows, who are happily still very much children of nature. The volumes which circulate most in the ward-room are undoubtedly those of the Dictionaire [sic] Larousse, which, apart from the instruction which it gives us in our isolation from the rest of the world, cuts short if it does not completely check, discussions which would otherwise threaten to be interminable.[105]

A library is important for all Antarctic expeditions and, even in these days of video recordings, provides an essential resource for getting through the polar winter. Not that the books are always used with discrimination; Laurence Gould, who went with Byrd on his first Antarctic expedition, has recounted how one of the pilots decided that, with the long winter night ahead, he would read through the *Encyclopaedia Britannica*. He gave up at ammonium tetrachloride with the remark: 'That damn book is of no use to a pilot!' Gould himself would have liked to have spent another winter down south just for the luxury of reading.[106] To return to Charcot; the *Pourquoi-*

Pas? expedition added greatly to Antarctic literature; its results, which included many maps and charts of great accuracy, filled twenty-eight volumes of published reports.

The British Graham Land Expedition of 1934–7, a private venture, was modest but extremely successful in extending knowledge of the Peninsula southwards. It was conceived in a cheerful evening's conversation on an expedition in the Arctic led by the young explorer Gino Watkins, who next day disappeared while on a lone excursion in a kayak, and was brought to realization by his friend John Rymill. Its ship the *Penola*, an old wooden Brittany fishing schooner, was sailed by the scientists of the expedition under the guidance of the only two professional seamen, the captain and chief engineer. A single-engine de Havilland Fox Moth was taken to make aerial surveys. First from a base on the Argentine Islands and then from the Debenham Islands further south in Marguerite Bay, reconnaisance was carried out which showed that the Peninsula is a peninsula and not cut off by a strait as had been suggested by the Antarctic aviator Hubert Wilkins. Much geological, glaciological and biological work was done – and all for a total cost of only £20,000 over the three years. The equipment was so meagre that the biologists had to make their own balance using a wooden beam poised on a pebble ground to a knife edge.[107]

Today there is a British station, Faraday, on the Argentine Islands, which is mainly a geophysical observatory concerned with the study of the upper atmosphere, including ozone measurements, geomagnetism and meteorology. These activities need take one no further outside the station than perhaps 100 metres to the meteorological screen, but it would be expecting too much of flesh and blood to confine Fids within such limits. At Faraday, as at other BAS stations, it is accepted that men should go on recreational trips, or 'jollies', provided that they are sensibly planned and clearly laid down safety regulations are observed. From Faraday the 8-kilometre (5-mile) trip north to Petermann Island, where the *Pourquoi-Pas?* wintered, is a pleasant way of filling in an afternoon. A Gemini (inflatable rubber dinghy with outboard) bounces off rocks and ice and, with a top speed of 25 knots, can get away quickly if bad weather threatens. Life-jackets are worn, of course, radio contact is maintained with base, and there is a refuge hut with provisions on the island in case of emergency. As one arrives, squads of gentoo penguins porpoise around the boat and those on land are all agog – nothing so exciting has happened around these parts for years. The presence of this penguin and the blue-eyed shag, neither of which get as far south anywhere else in Antarctica, is part of the justification for describing this region as the 'banana belt'. There is the interest of identifying the layout of Charcot's station and the scenery – this is at the south end of the Lemaire Channel – is magnificent.

In the winter, an expedition from Faraday out across the sea-ice to Petermann Island can be just as straightforward and rewarding. It was in August 1982 that such a trip went tragically wrong. Three men set off pulling equipment and provisions sufficient for an absence of considerably more than was needed for the two or three days they intended to stay there. After a journey of about four hours they arrived safely, but just before they intended to return a violent storm arose and broke up the sea-ice. They had to resign themselves to a prolonged stay, but they had adequate shelter with ample provisions and they were in radio contact with Faraday. After a month, during which the weather prevented rescue by boat, young sea-ice began to reform and, impatient to get back, the men evidently thought that it was worth investigating a return route. They had been trained in assessing the strength and stability of sea-ice. Exactly what happened will never be known, but a sea swell arose and they must have been caught as the new ice broke up, and died from drowning or exposure. Search by boat was impossible because of the weather and a search by air, mounted promptly from the Chilean base on the South Shetlands, found no trace of the party. Short of forbidding such expeditions altogether there appears to be no tightening of safety precautions that can prevent such accidents. It is a sense of adventure that leads men to go to the Antarctic and that there are risks is understood and accepted.

Further south is another large island, Adelaide. It was after a nightmare circumnavigation, during which he sighted the land mass of East Antarctica for the first time, that in 1832 John Biscoe of the firm of Enderby Brothers, approaching the Peninsula from the west, discovered an island which he named after Queen Adelaide. He described it thus:

Adelaide Island has a most imposing and beautiful appearance, with one high peak shooting up into the clouds, and occasionally appearing both above and below them, and a lower range of mountains extending about four miles, from north to south, having only a thin covering of snow on their summits, but towards their base buried in a field of snow and ice of the most dazzling brightness, which slopes down to the water, and terminates in a cliff of ten or twelve feet high, riven and splintered in every direction to an extent of two or three hundred yards from its edge.[108]

It was that field of snow and ice that later attracted the British Antarctic Survey to set up a base for air communications on Adelaide Island. The first site selected proved to be more often than not difficult to get at from the sea because of sea-ice, and crevasses had appeared in the runway on the ice-field. The construction of a new station at Rothera Point was completed in the summer of 1978–9. It is now the centre for BAS air operations. The planes, de Havilland Twin Otters, which fly down from Canada each season, use a snow runway from which to take off on radio echo-sounding and aeromagnetic surveys and to ferry field parties out to remote localities. These parties, often consisting of just one scientist with a field assistant skilled in the arts of navigation and survival, set up temporary camps from which excursions are made by skidoo – the 'tin dog' replacing the real dogs which were used not so long ago.

A runway on solid ground would be more satisfactory than the one on snow and allow larger planes to be used; at the time of writing the building of a gravel airstrip is being considered. This would enable a regular air bridge with the Falklands to be operated and make possible flights south as far as the Pole. Apart from those of finance and construction, there is a more serious problem to be considered, that of possible damage to the environment. There was furore over the building of a hard-rock air strip at the French Dumont d'Urville Station in Adélie Land and there may well be similar opposition from the international Antarctic community to one at Rothera. Against possible damage to plant and animal communities, which one hopes could be minimized, must be balanced the advantages of extending Antarctic work of environmental significance such as that on the ozone layer. Environmental problems are never in clear black and white.

The most nostalgic of the British stations on the Peninsula, now unoccupied but kept provisioned and in good repair – it is accepted that anyone in need may use the resources of an unoccupied base – is Stonington in Marguerite Bay. Stonington Island, named after the old whaling port in Connecticut, is a small island with access to the mainland of the Peninsula by a glacier bridge. It provides an excellent base and has been shared by American and British expeditions. The first of the latter, led by Surgeon-Commander E. W. Bingham, who had been on the British Graham Land Expedition, was sent out by the newly formed Falkland Islands Dependencies Survey in 1945.

Jennie's Lookout on Stonington Island is a bare rocky promontory with – presuming a summer's day in a good year – magnificent views over indigo sea set with icebergs to mountains jagged enough to show large exposures of colourful rock. A simple wooden cross on its highest point marks a mound of stones covering the bodies of two Fids who died in a blizzard in 1966. The Jennie who looked out was one of the first two women to overwinter in the Antarctic. It was a last-minute decision of Commander Finn Ronne, leader of the 1947–8 US Research Expedition, to take his wife and, as a companion for her, Jennie Darlington, the bride of his senior air pilot. For Jennie, needless to say, it was an unforgettable experience and it culminated in rescue from Stonington by ice-breaker just in time for her baby to be deprived of the distinction of being the first to be born within the Antarctic Circle. It was not an altogether idyllic honeymoon; there was dissension within the

Icebergs and blizzard (water-colour)

American expedition and, at first, hostility between Ronne and the British party under Bingham only a few hundred yards away. Jennie's description of her encounter with the British must be quoted:

> Shortly after we were settled ashore, I set out to explore my surroundings. Walking over the hill, I came upon the FIDS' tethering line.
>
> On our arrival several of the Britishers had been away from the base. Now one, obviously just back from the trail, was tying up his dogs. If he heard my approach the man gave no indication of it. After a quick, desultory glance he turned his back on me.
>
> In that wilderness, as far from conventional mores and civilization as it is possible to be, I stood nervously debating whether I should speak or take flight. The Britisher finished tethering the dogs and began to unload his sledge. Nobody said a word. I could have been a snow statue or a mirage.
>
> Then, pushing a shovel at me, he issued a clipped command. 'I say, hold this a moment, will you?'
>
> 'Certainly,' I answered automatically.
>
> At the sound of my voice the man started. He slowly straightened up from the sledge, turned, and stared at me, his eyes going from the end of my long green and white knitted stocking cap, from under which pigtails protruded, to the tips of my regulation boots. Then his eyes widened. His mouth dropped open. Astonishment, embarassment, and a certain confused fear flashed across his weather-beaten face.
>
> Involuntarily he reached out, grabbed the shovel, looked at it an instant, and then glanced back at me. Without another word he turned and fled to the British bunkhouse.
>
> While I stood considering Anglo-American relations, two men emerged from the hut, my acquaintance from the tethering line escorted by Tommy Thomson, the British Auster pilot. As though stalking a she-bear, they advanced within earshot. 'No need to take on so,' Thomson was saying. 'Just thought we'd have an absolute smasher waiting for you when you got back.'
>
> 'But a blonde, with pigtails,' gasped the man who'd been out on the trail.
>
> 'Say, old chap, you're pulling my leg.'
>
> Thomson was unable to contain himself any longer. At the sight of his friend's panic-stricken face he burst into peals of laughter. 'Come now,' he choked, taking the shaken man by the arm and propelling him towards me. 'It's Mrs Darlington from the American camp. I'll introduce you.' With a wonderful example of British understatement he concluded gallantly, 'Do forgive the chap for losing his manners. It isn't often that we see a beautiful woman in the Antarctic.'

Any woman, I thought, even one in a parka and pigtails and a coating of lanolin, must look beautiful to a man who hasn't seen one in two years! Dr. Butson's relief at finding me real was also beautiful. Like a man encountering an orange trail marker after being lost, he said 'Thank God!' In heartfelt tones he concluded, 'I thought I'd gone round the bend. I do apologize. After mucking about on a glacier for several months I mistook you for a mirage.'[109]

After that, Jennie seems to have got on better with the Fids than she did with her compatriots.

Of course, other women had preceded Jennie Darlington into Antarctica. The first to cross the Antarctic Circle had been a castaway on Campbell Island, south of New Zealand, who, together with three male companions, was rescued by the *Eliza Scott* and *Sabrina*, two vessels belonging to the Enderby brothers, on their way south in 1839 on a voyage of exploration. The Balleny Islands were discovered and the mainland of Antarctica glimpsed, but on their return the *Sabrina* was lost in a ferocious storm. Evidently the woman was aboard her and so passed into history, nameless. Norwegian whaling captains at the beginning of this century took their womenfolk with them on their voyages south almost as a matter of course. The Four Ladies Bank discovered by the *Thorshaven* in 1937 at 67°35'S 77°30'E bears witness to this and Mrs Mikkelsen, a Norwegian whaling captain's wife, was the first woman to set foot on the continent; this was at the Vestfold Hills in February 1935.

The nations seem to have different attitudes to women in Antarctica. Like the Norwegians, the Russians have seen no difficulty in taking women south. Considering the bulk and headscarves supposed to be characteristic of their female workers it may ungallantly be thought that for them there is no problem. Nevertheless, it is a fact that photographs of one Svetlana are still to be seen around the British base on Signy Island and the legend persists that the base commander at the time of her visit did himself a serious mischief in attempting to blow farewell kisses from the vantage point of the flagstaff when the Russian research vessel departed. The Argentinians have taken women south for the patently political purpose of having children born in Antarctica. Women have worked at US Antarctic stations for some time now and that this has quickly acquired an air of normality perhaps depends on the American propensity to establish their way of life wherever they find themselves, cocooning it against the alien world outside. Americans go down to Antarctica as cooks, mechanics, radio operators, doctors or scientists and stick to these roles, a woman carrying out her job much as she would do back home without being put into any very different relationship with her male companions or necessarily having to face the full rigours of the Antarctic environment. Other nations, including both those long established in the Antarctic, such as Australia and New Zealand, and more recent arrivals, such as India, routinely include women in their expeditions.

The United Kingdom, on the other hand, has been the last of the major Antarctic powers to have women in its field parties. This seemingly unenlightened attitude was not adopted because of any particular susceptibilities that, from what has been related above, it may be thought that Fids have, but it is based on practical considerations. It is a sound principle in the Antarctic not to change anything that works well unless there are compelling reasons to do so and over the course of time the British Antarctic Survey has evolved an ethos based on small all-male communities which has been extremely successful both in terms of harmony within the group and scientific productivity. On a British base, as has already been described, each man is expected to undertake any task that may be required of him regardless of his specialization and calculated risks are taken in avoiding too much inhibition of the spirit of adventure. The introduction of women might be a spanner in these nicely adjusted works. The approach of the Survey in taking on women has therefore been cautious but there are already a few female Fids working on its research vessels and no doubt their numbers will increase and they will soon be accepted without comment or fuss in land stations.[110]

Women are at least as well able as men to withstand polar conditions and, even in the Antarctic, the fitness of an individual for a particular piece of work should override the accident of sex. Beyond this, it is quite unjust that men should keep such a beautiful and unique part of the world to themselves.

Perhaps it might be argued that the attachment of the Fid to his dogs is the result of his being deprived of female society. Once the British had become convinced of the value of the dog-sledge and had mastered the art of dog-handling, they became leading exponents of this form of transport in the Antarctic and used it extensively until as recently as 1974. Jennie Darlington, who herself became adept at driving huskies, has given us a picture of its heyday:

> When the trail party from the British base at Hope Bay arrived, I sensed the time-honoured romance and appeal of long polar journeys.
>
> That day in 1947 those of us watching, as team after team poured down off the glacier, saw a sight that may never be seen again. Six dog teams and ten men who had travelled hundreds of miles exemplified an old fashioned art that may soon (due to the current-day steam-heated exploration programmes) belong to the polar past.
>
> In silence broken only by the creak of runners on snow the huskies swept down off the glacier. The men's faces were fine-drawn, gaunt, wind-

Sea-ice and icebergs (water-colour)

burned almost to blackness. The dogs, though still galloping and gallant, were obviously tired, sinking down into the snow to sleep on arrival. Equipment was worn from hard use. Windproofs were torn and weathered.

Yet as they came down, the dogs waving their tails like plumed banners, their coats rippling like multicoloured waves against the whiteness, an awed stillness descended on us. Matched step by step by magnified blue shadows, the weary dogs, the bearded men, signified the pioneer concepts of strength, simplicity, and survival.[111]

The sledges, of a design orginating with the great Arctic explorer, Fridtjof Nansen, are built to give maximum strength with minimum weight, of selected ash or hickory, the pieces being lashed together, rather than screwed, to give flexibility over uneven ground. Like boats, they are given individual names. They remain essentially the same although now pulled more often by skidoos (motor toboggans or snow-scooters) rather than by dogs. The dogs, huskies, descendants of the wolf but bred in Antarctica by the British for many generations, weigh between 39 and 43 kilograms (85 and 95 pounds) and can each pull a load of 50 kilograms (110 pounds) for a journey lasting 40 days on about 1 kilogram (2–3 lbs) of pemmican or dried fish per day. Curled into a ball, they keep warm buried in snow, they prefer eating snow to drinking water and, when in good condition, they give every indication of enjoying pulling.[112]

The dog sledge remains the safest form of transport over unknown snow-fields. With the dogs attached to individual traces so that they can fan out, as is the British way, weight is more evenly distributed and if a dog goes down a crevasse the others can jump aside. Dogs in pairs on a single centre trace in the American fashion can present a heavy and complicated tangle if they go down but obviously, in country with trees where this technique originated, this was the only possible arrangement. The dogs themselves are often acute in recognizing unsafe snow bridges. *In extremis*, dog can be fed on dog and man on dog. But not the least of the advantages of dogs is their value for maintaining the morale of the men. Huskies are affectionate animals and close bonds develop between them and their masters. They are individuals and on a long monotonous journey their social relations provide interest, and the occasional fight. Their eerie habit of howling in chorus, which they do when a team of their fellows or a ship departs from base or for other more obscure canine reasons, is something to be remembered with nostalgia. Fids are unashamedly sentimental about their dogs, most of their stations still keep one or two, even though they do not work, and, rightly, there is a special prayer for them: 'Look kindly, O Lord, on these Thy creatures for we are dependent on them and they, with us, are utterly dependent on Thee'.

South from Stonington, the coasts of the Peninsula become increasingly decked with shelf-ice and beset with pack-ice. On a clear day the mountains of Alexander Island, 150 kilometres (90 miles) away, are visible as one rounds Nenny Island after leaving Stonington but George VI Sound, which separates Alexander Island from the Peninsula mainland, is inaccessible to ships, being perennially blocked by an ice-shelf. On its western shore at Fossil Bluff is a small BAS station, established as an advance base for earth sciences, occupied only during the summer and supplied by air. The name was given with reason; sediments there contain enormous quantities of fossil ammonites, gasteropods, other molluscs and worms of lower Cretaceous age.

An odd thing at nearby Ablation Point is that there are lakes which are freshwater but tidal. These have arisen by the damming of the end of a valley by the ice shelf, holding the fresh water floating on top of the denser seawater beneath the shelf. The top layer has rather sparse freshwater algae and invertebrates, but marine fish are found in the bottom waters. Those who named the features of Alexander Island were musically inclined for, amongst others, it has a Beethoven Peninsula, a Bach Ice Shelf, a Berlioz Point, Staccato Peaks and a Sibelius Glacier. One feels that Sibelius, who drew his inspiration from the sub-Arctic, would have particularly appreciated this distinction, but that Bach would have been just bewildered. In any case the size of Bach Ice Shelf is trifling by Antarctic standards, and to look at these remarkable structures it will be best to move east across the Peninsula to those in the Weddell Sea.

Sno-cat tracks near Halley Base, Brunt Ice Shelf (oil)

Chapter Eight

The Ice Shelves

THE SOUTHERN PART of the Weddell Sea is covered over with a shelf of ice about the same size as France and varying in thickness from about 200 metres (660 feet) at its seaward, floating edge, to 600 metres (2000 feet) where it joins the inland ice sheet. It is divided by Berkner Island into a larger western part, the Ronne Ice Shelf and a smaller eastern part, the Filchner Ice Shelf. On the opposite side of the continent in the embayment of the Ross Sea is the even more enormous Ross Ice Shelf, the Barrier of Scott and Shackleton. Other, smaller, ice shelves occur around Antarctica and altogether about a third of its coastline is occupied by them and they amount to 7 per cent of the total ice-covered area. The ice shelf is a peculiarly Antarctic phenomenon, not frequent in the Arctic. It is a reasonably stable and permanent structure and experience has shown that it is practical to set up stations on ice shelves. Byrd's succession of Little Americas were on the Ross Ice Shelf and one of the best known of the present stations, Halley, is on the Brunt Ice Shelf, a mere 65 kilometres (40 miles) across, in the Weddell Sea. Why this particular station should be so called needs some explanation.

Edmond Halley hits the headlines every seventy-six years with the return of the comet which bears his name, but he deserves better than this. He was one of the world's most wide-ranging scientists, for besides his justly famous astronomical work he carried out various kinds of geophysical studies, laid a firm basis for the theory of annuities and life insurance, invented diving bells that worked and translated mathematical treatises from the Arabic.[4] Moreover he possessed 'a vein of gaiety and good humour

171

which neither his abstracted speculations, the infirmities of old age, nor the palsy itself which seized him some years before his death, could impair'. However, there are more particular reasons why the Royal Society should have named after him the base it set up in 1956 on the Brunt Ice Shelf for the International Geophysical Year and why later a British Antarctic Survey station should have taken over the name.

Halley was the son of a soap manufacturer in the time of the great plague and so was able to devote himself to science without financial worries. One of his interests was in magnetism and especially the variation of magnetic declination over the globe – obviously a matter of importance for navigation. Such was his standing as a scientist that a ship, the *Paramore*, was built specially for him to carry out a survey of magnetic declination and make determinations of longitude. What is more, the Admiralty made him, a civilian, her commander. There was some delay because he became involved at Isaac Newton's behest as deputy-controller of the mint at Chester and then the Russian Tsar, Peter the Great, who was visiting London to learn about shipbuilding, was lent the *Paramore* to practise his seamanship. There is a story, probably apocryphal, of the Tsar amusing himself by trundling Halley on a wheelbarrow through the hedges of John Evelyn's immaculately kept garden at Deptford. In due course, however, Halley successfully captained cruises in the Atlantic in 1698–1700, producing a chart of magnetic declination which remained in use for a hundred years. On his second voyage he reached latitude 52°30'S just to the north of South Georgia, which he missed discovering by about 100 nautical miles, but he did penetrate south of the Antarctic Convergence among the icebergs.

This was the first voyage ever to be undertaken specifically for a scientific purpose and his venture into Antarctic waters was deliberate. Beyond this, it was his insistence on the importance of observing the transit of Venus, as a means of determining the distance of the Earth from the Sun, that launched James Cook on his exploration of southern waters, and it was on his work on terrestrial magnetism and the behaviour and cause of trade winds that the foundations of the science of geophysics were laid. It has been geophysics, from the time of the *Erebus* and *Terror* expedition of 1839 to the International Geophysical Year in 1957, which has provided the main impetus for Antarctic exploration and research. One feels that, were Halley alive today, he would not only be chairing committees planning Antarctic research but would be thoroughly at home among Fids around the bar in their base. His shade may be nevertheless bemused to contemplate his portrait in the place of honour in a building sunk in a waste of ice floating on the Antarctic sea.

Halley Station is supplied by sea; it takes about five days' steaming, given good ice conditions, for BAS's RRS *Bransfield* to get there from the South Sandwich Islands. It is about six hours flight by Twin Otter from Rothera and two and a half hours from McMurdo by Hercules. Approaching from the sea the first indication of the Brunt Ice Shelf is 'ice-blink' – white glare from the underside of clouds, contrasting sharply with the dark grey of 'water-sky', clouds over the sea – and this is followed by the appearance of a white line across the horizon. Nearer, the shelf is seen as a surprisingly regular white cliff usually some 30 metres (100 feet) in height, fronting a level or gently undulating plain of snow.

Snowfall is actually rather low, below 5 centimetres (2 inches) water equivalent per annum, over most of the Antarctic continent. However, snow has had perhaps 30 million years to accumulate there and now the ice formed from it has an average thickness of 2.3 kilometres (1.4 miles); over large areas its weight has pressed the land surface down below sea level. Being plastic under pressure, the ice flows outwards under its own weight, slowly, like a pile of freshly mixed cement. A particle of snow falling at the spot furthest from any sea may take 100,000 years to travel the 1900 kilometres (1200 miles) to the edge of the ice sheet. It moves more rapidly, more than 300 metres (1000 feet) a year, where aided by the slope of the land, sliding over the rock where pressure causes melting. Only the biggest of obstacles can divert the flow and huge glaciers are formed where mountain ranges present a barrier.

At the edge of the continent, glaciers and ice streams break off ('calve') and form icebergs, which are dispersed by the sea, but where ice streams converge, as in a large bay, they may coalesce to form a solid slab, an ice shelf, floating out over the sea. Ice shelves are not formed in the Arctic because, apart from the much less extensive ice-cap, the necessary configurations of the coastline are not present. As these shelves spread slowly over the sea, pieces break off from the seaward edge to form the characteristic tabular bergs described on page 113.[34] There was much discussion among the early explorers about the origin of tabular bergs but once an ice shelf had been seen their formation was obvious. James Savage, the armourer on the *Erebus*, whom we have quoted before, had no doubts about this:

> The Fragments as i call the floating Islands though Large Enough to build London on their Summit must through a Long Succession of years have parted from the Barrier they never could accumulate to Such an Enormous hight otherwise.[25]

An ice shelf is not a location on which to build for posterity, but it moves sufficiently slowly and calving is sufficiently predictable to allow the establishment of semi-permanent bases. The chief difficulty is that buildings become buried by drifting snow and sink in the ice, eventually to be crushed by pressure. Twenty-five years after being built, the first Halley base was some 20 metres (60 feet) down in the ice, mangled and inaccessible, part of it having floated out to sea in an iceberg. In 1955, when the US ice-breaker *Atka* visited the Bay of Whales, the spot where Amundsen had built his base Framheim and Byrd his Little Americas, she found herself 16 kilometres (10 miles) inland according to her navigator's reckoning. He had not made a mistake; a huge section of the Ross Ice Shelf had calved away, taking the Bay of Whales with it. From a helicopter a row of tent poles marking Little America IV was seen to terminate abruptly at the shelf edge and below it a tent hung from the cliff face. A dark line 2.3 metres ($7\frac{1}{2}$ feet) below the edge marked where the surface of 1947 had accumulated dirt and rubbish.

Long before it gets into such a state, a base can only be entered down a shaft, becoming ever more a fire hazard; joists buckle and trickles of melt water appear. The first British Antarctic Survey building at Halley remained habitable for seven years; the next, which was built within a tube of corrugated steel, lasted ten years. The latest is protected by flexible plywood tubes, 9 metres (30 feet) in diameter and 30–40 metres (100–130 feet) long, constructed of interlocking insulated panels in sections with sliding junctions to give more flexibility. Each tube houses a two-storey block of rooms with wide stairways and extendable access shafts to the surface, and in it up to twenty men can live and work comfortably almost in ignorance, if they wish, of the weather above. After only five years its replacement was being discussed. Even while it remains habitable it cannot be described as a fixed abode, for satellite observations show that it is being carried by the ice at a rate of nearly 750 metres (2500 feet) a year just south of west.

Clearly such a base cannot be put near the edge of the ice shelf but must be a few miles inland, safe from all but the largest break-outs. It must at the same time be as accessible as possible from the sea, near a stretch of shelf edge which is free of pack-ice in the summer and to which a ship can be moored to unload stores. The edge of an ice shelf, although constantly breaking up, may have persistent features determined by the direction of ice flows and islands underneath it. One such feature is the Bay of Whales, another is Mobster Creek – named after a dog team of past years – on the Brunt Ice Shelf. Here the ice cliff is interrupted by a wide gulley containing sea-ice with a snow slope going gently up to the top of the shelf. In a good year, a 100-metre (325-foot) long research vessel can lie snugly alongside the edge of the sea-ice within the creek, protected by ice cliffs fore and aft.

On arrival, RRS *Bransfield* gently noses up to the ice in one corner of Mobster Creek and down a rope ladder over her bows Fids swarm to join those already waiting on the ice to get in ice-anchors as quickly as possible. When the bows are secure, the ship is warped round to lie up to the ice edge. Then, without pause for any more than hasty welcomes, exchange of news or admiration of the scenery, unloading must begin, for at any time a storm may blow up or ice break away. Oil drums and other stores are loaded onto

Interior of ice cave (oil)

cargo sledges and towed away by Sno-cat with no dilly-dallying. An artist, of course, has licence, and David Smith was able to record such a scene:

I found it very stimulating in spite of the cold (I had to work with gloves on) to tackle in oils the lively subject of *Bransfield* unloading supplies for the base. To capture the spirit of such a subject one must, of course, paint it on the spot. The red ship towered above the sea ice, the cranes clattered as they swung to and fro. The Fids and crew in their bright-coloured clothing hammered the wedges between the heavy barrels of oil to fix them firmly on the sledges. The Sno-cats reversed in a flurry of snow as they hooked up to the sledges with their sixteen-barrel loads, and then away to base. All this, as an example of efficient, purposeful teamwork gave the stimulus for the painting. Standing in one place for a long time while working, I was surprised to find how my body weight and warmth caused my feet to melt the ice quite rapidly. To prevent myself sinking, it was necessary to procure a wooden plank from the ship to stand on and distribute my weight.

(Diary of David Smith)

In good weather, unloading may be completed in four days. In a bad year things may be much more difficult; 1973 was one of these, when the ice in Mobster Creek broke up during unloading and a quick search had to be made for an alternative site. This had to be on the nearest stretch of low ice cliff and there was only just enough room to operate the ship's crane. More trouble was to come because, as Sir Vivian Fuchs recounts, the ice:

had made yet another attack on *Bransfield*. Work over for the day shift, those on board were resting or watching a film when there was a monstrous crash and the ship heeled over on her beam ends. Three hundred feet of the ice cliff against which she was lying had fallen, crushing flat 150 feet of the bulwarks, and leaving a pile of ice blocks fifteen feet high on the foredeck. A hasty visual check showed one man missing, presumably somewhere underneath the grotesque ice pile.

Frantically everyone seized an implement, rushed out and started chopping, heaving, digging their hearts out, praying that somehow he had escaped serious injury. It was a long time before a more thorough count revealed that the victim they sought so strenuously had apparently changed his clothes and unrecognised, he too was busily digging for all he was worth, searching for himself.[113]

The next year brought problems of a different sort when the only possible unloading site was 65 kilometres (40 miles) from the base.

Plodding along the line of empty oil drums which mark the safe route to the base, one gets a feel – but certainly only the faintest sensation – of the heroic age of Antarctic exploration. The ice shelf, the 'bondu' to Fids, stretches indefinitely into the distance, its sameness only varied by crevasses. These are cracks which open up when the ice is under tensile stress, produced when the flow is altered by meeting a rocky obstruction, perhaps, or another ice stream. They vary in width from a few inches to chasms which could engulf a battleship and may be so deep as to disappear into blackness below. If one is able to contemplate it with equanimity, their beauty is a perfection of sculpted surfaces and crystalline embellishment illumined in sapphire light. Snow cornices grow out from the edges and form bridges across them. Whether or not these bridges will carry his weight is one of the chief preoccupations of the traveller across the shelf. Apart from crevasses, the only natural features of the shelf surface are 'sastrugi', the word being Russian not Fid in derivation, denoting the irregular ridges in the snow surface produced by wind erosion and drifting.

In a snow flurry one's universe contracts into the oval frame of the opening of one's anorak hood with, at the top, the rhythmic intrusion of the heels of the man in front, and below that the blue markings of the snow surface moving beneath one's own feet. A 'white-out', when light becomes completely diffused between snow surface and sky so that horizon and all contrasts disappear, can be terrifying. This is the ultimate Antarctic, a blankness which only those with exceptional mental reserves can survive for long. Admiral Richard Byrd, the father of American Antarctic exploration, is the only man who has voluntarily faced it alone for a protracted period. During his second expedition, in 1933–6, he elected to winter by himself at a temporary weather station established 198 kilometres (123 miles) inland from his main base, Little America, on the Ross Ice Shelf. Of course, he had snug quarters below the ice surface with books and radio contact with Little America. For a few weeks all went well; he was able to describe it as one of the greatest and most satisfying periods of his life. Here is his description of a morning at the beginning of winter.

> You stand on the Barrier, and simply look and listen and feel. The morning may be compounded of an unfathomable, tantalizing fog in which you stumble over sastrugi you can't see, and detour past obstructions that don't exist, and take your bearings from tiny bamboo markers that loom as big as telephone poles and hang suspended in space. On such a day, I could swear that the instrument shelter was as big as an ocean liner. On one such day I saw the blank north-eastern sky become filled with the most magnificent Barrier coast I have ever seen, true in every line and faced with cliffs several thousand feet tall. A mirage, of course. Yet, a man who had never seen such things would have taken oath that it was real. The afternoon may be so clear that you dare not make a sound, lest it fall in

pieces. And on such a day I have seen the sky shatter like a broken goblet, and dissolve into iridescent tipsy fragments – ice crystals falling across the face of the sun. And once in the golden downpour a slender column of platinum leaped up from the horizon, clean through the sun's core; a second luminous shadow formed horizontally through the sun, making a perfect cross. Presently two minature suns, green and yellow in colour, flipped simultaneously to the ends of each arm. These are parhelia, the most dramatic of all refraction phenomena; nothing is lovelier.[114]

He had several narrow escapes in blizzards but the unanticipated danger was that the ventilation of his hut was inadequate and slowly he was poisoned by carbon monoxide from his stove. He did not let the main base know that all was not well, fearing to put lives at risk if a rescue was attempted in the depth of winter. Eventually it was realized that he was ill and, after several attempts, a rescue mission reached the advanced base but it was two months before he recovered enough to be taken back to Little America.

In the waste of the ice shelf the sight of Halley Station at the end of its avenue of oil drums – a little like the line of sarsens leading to the stone circles of Avebury – offers no obvious welcome. Apart from radio masts and what look like large packing cases, one of which displays a London underground sign, which are the entrances to the shafts down to the buildings, there is little to see. A signpost points to places such as the South Pole (1606 kilometres – 998 miles), McMurdo Station (2834 kilometres – 1761 miles) and London (14,275 kilometres – 8870 miles). The nearest human habitation is the Argentine base, General Belgrano, 438 kilometres (272 miles) away to the south-east.

Life down below is comfortable, if claustrophobic. In the lounge there are pictures of ships, penguins, groups of Fids and a photograph recording the first visit of a woman to the base – Ella Woodfield who accompanied her husband, the captain of the *Bransfield*, in 1974 – with her three companions in dinner jackets and black ties confronting a couple of emperor penguins. The central feature of the lounge, the bar, would be well worthy of any pub back home, apart from a relative paucity of bottles. BAS provides a basic ration of alcohol and Fids may take their own additional supplies which, on the whole, are used sensibly, usually being saved up for Saturday nights. During the summer, Halley may be visited by an occasional plane or ship but otherwise is as isolated as one can be in this modern world. The moment when the relief vessel draws away from Mobster Creek leaving a small group of men rapidly dwindling to dots in a white immensity, is poignant enough even if a piper playing a lament is not always present.

The isolation becomes acute if there is an accident. In 1967, two men from Halley on a man-hauling expedition doing physiological research became overdue and after 28 hours were found, both injured from falling over a 9-metre (30-foot) cliff in a white-out, one, the base doctor as it happened, with a seriously injured spine. The Fids managed to get an X-ray machine working and the principal patient had to interpret the photographs for himself. When, back in London, it was realized that his condition was serious, American help was enlisted and two ski-equipped Hercules flew over from McMurdo. In about twenty hours after leaving Halley the patient had been flown across the continent and, after a refuelling stop at McMurdo, on to hospital in Christchurch, New Zealand. At 9000 kilometres (5600 miles) this is probably the longest rescue flight in Antarctic history. He made a complete recovery, thanks to the speed and efficiency of the rescue operation. This story illustrates not only the unquestioning and generous help which Antarctic nations, particularly the Americans, give each other in emergencies, but also the truth of the maxim that troubles never come singly, for at the same time a volcanic eruption on Deception Island was destroying the Chilean base and its occupants were seeking refuge with the British.[83]

To put an elaborate and expensive installation in this remote and inconvenient place requires particularly good scientific justification. This rests on Halley being a geophysical observatory placed at a spot ideally situated for studying the upper atmosphere and geospace, that is, space in the immediate neighbourhood of the earth. The station is in a sector of the continent most distant from the magnetic pole and lies on the outer edge of the auroral zone encircling it. This is where the magnetic field lines which run between the north and south poles curve downwards into the earth. These field lines act as wave-guides for radio signals, produced by thunderstorms, which are funnelled down to Halley as 'whistlers', distinctive sequences of falling pitch. Much can be deduced from whistlers about what is going on in the upper atmosphere. The information obtained is of global significance and is useful in, for example, radio communications and space research.[115]

Much other research goes on at Halley, but there is no need to go into technicalities here except to touch on the dramatic business of the 'hole in the ozone layer'. Ozone present in trace amounts in the atmosphere is our main effective screen against damaging intensities of ultra-violet radiation from the sun. Its concentration depends on a balance between formation and destruction in the upper layers of the atmosphere and it happens that chloro-fluorocarbons, man-made chemicals widely used in industry as aerosol propellants and in refrigeration equipment, among other things, promote the destructive processes. It was realized some time ago that accumulation of these gases in the atmosphere might lead to thinning of the ozone layer and so programmes of observations on atmospheric ozone were set up by Britain and the United States. No very definite cause for worry was found until

1984 when British Antarctic Survey scientists reported a remarkable thinning of the ozone layer over Halley in the Antarctic spring. This was found using traditional methods in which the total ozone content of the air column is determined from the ground and the vertical profile of concentrations is obtained with an ozone-sonde, a balloon-borne device from which information is radioed back to base. A much more sophisticated system carried on the US Nimbus 7 satellite failed to detect this 'hole' because it had been programmed to discount as erroneous any measurements departing widely from what was to be expected. It delights scientific individualists, but not organizing committees, to draw a moral from this.

In more precise terms, the 'hole' is a depletion of the total ozone in the stratospheric vortex formed over Antarctica during the winter. Its existence was quickly confirmed by re-examination of the satellite data and comparisons of observations onwards from 1979 have shown a progressive spreading of the hole. A 5 per cent change in ozone over a century had been thought to be adverse; this was 50 per cent, albeit locally, in only ten years, but a perhaps more alarming aspect was that the sudden depletion could not be explained. A large-scale international investigation using specially equipped aircraft, including a modified U2 spy plane capable of reaching the centre of the ozone hole 18 kilometres (11 miles) above the earth, carried out in the Antarctic spring of 1987, seemed to confirm that chlorine derived from chlorofluorocarbons is implicated. Until more is learnt it is sensible to take precautions. Sun-bathers in Australia, who are nearest to the 'hole', have become almost fanatic in applying protective oils to guard against skin cancer and there was international agreement in the autumn of 1987 to cut back the production of chlorofluorocarbons and similar substances – making history as the first global pollution control agreement. So an esoteric bit of science at Halley Station has affected, surely for good, the lives of us all.[116]

An ice shelf, apart from the occasional intruding skua or human, is a biological desert. Even snow algae are not found since temperatures are too low to permit the freeze-thaw cycles on which these organisms depend. Amazingly, however, there is some life below the shelf. Samples obtained by drilling through the Ross Ice Shelf at a point more than 400 kilometres (250 miles) away from the open sea have been found to contain low numbers of bacteria and sparse shrimp-like animals. In this situation, plant photosynthesis is impossible because no light penetrates and it seems highly unlikely that organic particles could be carried in the water under the shelf as far as this so there is the problem of what these organisms use as food. The only possibility seems to be the small amounts of organic materials dissolved in seawater, which bacteria might utilize and then themselves become food for the animals. Observations show that water under the shelf may be replaced every six years or so, making this the merest trickle of support for life.

Biology at Halley may be extremely short on species to study but it is high in appeal since nearby on the ice edge there is a colony of more than 10,000 breeding pairs of emperor penguins. These splendid birds are the largest living penguins, standing up to 1 metre (3 feet) high and weighing up to 46 kilograms (100 pounds). They have a blue-black back and wings and a white shirt-front shading into yellow above with orange ear-patches. In demeanour as well as appearance they are truly imperial; their movements are deliberate and stately – it would be easy to choreograph them into the entry of the peers in *Iolanthe* – contrasting with the noisy bustle of those slum dwellers, the smaller penguins. With human beings they are unafraid but aloof. Emperor penguins feed on squid and fish, diving for them to depths of as much as 250 metres (820 feet) and staying under for as long as eighteen minutes. They breed on the ice and have to overcome the difficulty that, because the sufficiency of food necessary for young birds is only available briefly in the summer, the incubation of eggs must be done in the depths of winter. This is the job of the male; there is no nest and the single egg is balanced across the top of his feet and covered with a fold of warm abdominal skin. While the females head north to open water, the males stay put, living on their fat.

The incubating emperor may have to withstand temperatures down to $-48°C$ ($-54°F$) and is superbly designed to do so. Being large, the surface from which heat can be lost is relatively small and it is insulated with double-layered and high density feathers. Heat exchange devices reduce loss through flippers, feet and nasal passages to a minimum. There is also an effective behavioural mechanism; the incubating birds go into a dense huddle, sometimes of as many as 5000 birds, in which there is a slow circulation with birds to the windward moving along the flank of the huddle and then, when they reach the lee side, back into the centre, until the movement of the whole mass again exposes them at the rear. After two months, the eggs begin to hatch and the females return to feed the chicks on partly digested food from their crops. Released from their ordeal, the males go off to sea to recuperate and to return with a further load of food for the chicks. As the ice edge breaks back towards the colony, parental fishing forays are more frequent and by summer the chicks, which have now lost most of their dense grey down and have become smaller and less colourful, but nevertheless adorable, versions of their parents, are ready for independence. When the sea ice breaks beneath them, they travel with it north into the Weddell Sea, feeding on the abundant plankton. In spite of everything, things work out remarkably well in average and good years, with about three-quarters of the birds raising a chick to independence and the emperor penguin colonies at Halley Bay and elsewhere seem to be maintaining themselves satisfactorily. These are the native heirs to Antarctica.[117]

Icescape, Weddell Sea (oil)

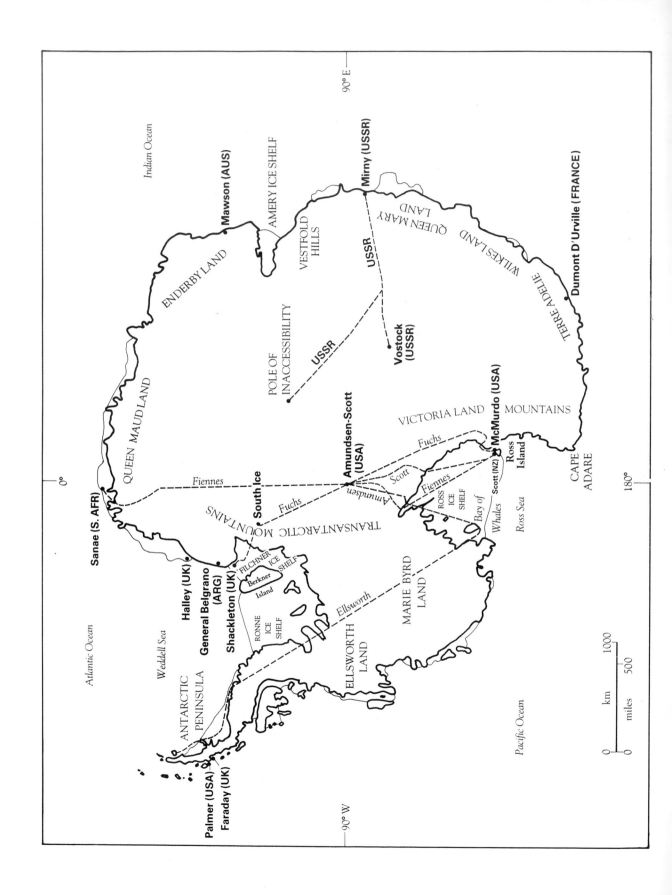

Chapter Nine

The Continent of Antarctica

I T USED TO BE SAID that we know more about the face of the moon than about the geography of Antarctica. This is no longer true; the map of the continent is criss-crossed with traverses, both over the snow and airborne, most of its area has been photographed from the air, satellites scan it and, although there are still vast regions that have never been visited, we can make shrewd guesses as to what is there. During the heroic age no more than a thin sliver of the continent from the Ross Sea to the Pole was explored but this sufficed to identify the chief topographical features – ice shelf, mountain range, glaciers, ice-free dry valleys and the polar plateau. The Byrd expeditions began the systematic filling in of blank spaces and the aeroplane gave overall views of what was there. The crossing of the continent dreamt of by Shackleton became something of no particular merit from the point of view of mapping or science, but it had a symbolic significance as the last major journey possible in the south polar region which had not yet been done.

The idea of another attempt at a trans-Antarctic expedition was hatched when a three-day blizzard enforced a lie-up on a two-man expedition from the British base at Stonington. At the south end of King George VI Sound, about 720 kilometres (450 miles) from base, they were at the limit of the range of an unsupported dog-sledge party. When re-reading their two books and the labels on tins of food had palled, the two, Vivian Fuchs and Raymond Adie, fell to discussing the geology of the interior of the continent and to sketching the logistics of the 3200-kilometre (2000-mile) journey that would be necessary in studying it. With a journey of that length, it

The continent of Antarctica showing the positions of some of the main scientific stations and the routes of some traverses.

185

would be more sensible to go right across the continent than to retrace one's steps. Later Fuchs discussed the idea with James Wordie, who had been chief of the scientific staff on Shackleton's *Endurance* expedition, and who was now Master of St John's College, Cambridge, and a power in Antarctic affairs. Things moved slowly but with the outcome that in 1955, six years after the idea was conceived, the advance party set off. The plan, after various possibilities had been considered, was essentially similar to Shackleton's. The crossing party would set out from a base on the Filchner Ice Shelf in the Weddell Sea and finish up in the Ross Sea area, going via the Pole and depending during the second part of its journey on depots laid by a support party working in from the Ross Sea end. It was to be a Commonwealth Expedition and received support from the governments of New Zealand, South Africa, Australia, the United Kingdom and from bodies such as the Royal Geographical Society and industry. Fuchs became its leader.[118]

The first task in Antarctica was to establish a base on the Filchner Ice Shelf and MV *Theron*, loaded to capacity with stores, a Sno-cat, an Auster aircraft and fuel for them, was dispatched to do this. She was only the second ship to enter the Weddell Sea since the *Endurance* and was not to escape unscathed – a twisted rudder was only restored to a usable condition by the desperate expedient of going hard astern against solid ice to bend it back. Shackleton Base was established, almost exactly where Shackleton himself had intended to put his, and the advance party was left to put up its buildings. A large amount of stores had perforce been left on the sea-ice and after a storm the advance party found that all their coal and much food and fuel had gone out to sea. A temporary dwelling was constructed out of the crate which had contained the Sno-cat and the party survived. Erection of the main hut went on slowly under conditions about as hard as they could be. In the next season the main crossing party sailed south, sharing MV *Magga Dan* with the Royal Society Antarctic Expedition going to occupy their base at Halley Bay – quite separately from the trans-Antarctic venture, plans for the International Geophysical Year had developed, resulting in activities all over Antarctica that will be described in Chapter Ten.

From Shackleton, an advanced base, South Ice, 480 kilometres (300 miles) towards the Pole, was set up entirely by air, a single-engined Otter making twenty flights carrying a tonne each time. This base was occupied throughout the following winter by three men who carried out a programme of meteorological and glaciological work. Conditions were more severe there, at an altitude of 1350 metres (4430 feet), than at Shackleton, lowest temperatures being $-57.3°C$ $(-71.1°F)$ and $-53°C$ $(-63.4°F)$, and mean wind speeds in May 1957 30.2 and 17.8 knots, respectively. A reconnaissance party under Fuchs with four vehicles – three Weasels (tracked cargo carriers) and a Sno-cat – often roped together as if they were climbers, worked out a tortuous route over horrendously crevassed ice up to South Ice.

Vehicles were constantly breaking through the snow bridges spanning crevasses and extrication was a dangerous operation taking up to six hours and the exercise of infinite patience and skill in finding safe ground on which to manoeuvre. On one occasion a Weasel driven by Fuchs was left suspended by its tow-bar at the rear and only the tip of its forward tracks at the front across an abyss, apparently bottomless and widening downwards in all directions. Fuchs recorded laconically: 'I climbed out safely enough, after the others had taken the photographs they wanted', and the Weasel was safely hauled out after some careful preliminary thoughts. At another time, as Ken Blaiklock, the surveyor, was kneeling examining a hole and chatting to a companion, the snow beneath him fell away leaving him suspended above a chasm by the ends of his skis. Meanwhile, geological parties were investigating, not without incident, the two mountain groups, the Theron Mountains and the Shackleton Range, which had been discovered.

The Ross Sea party, which had become a New Zealand responsibility under the leadership of Sir Edmund Hillary of Everest fame, had established Scott Base near to the US McMurdo Station. This was to be a joint Trans-Antarctic–International Geophysical Year base and the close association with the Americans was going to be valuable. A route was prospected up the Skelton Glacier on to the plateau and depot-laying along the route to the Pole was begun by Beaver aircraft. Hillary and three companions tried out their modified Ferguson farm tractors by following the route of 'the worst journey in the world' taken by Wilson, Bowers and Cherry-Garrard to collect emperor penguin eggs from Cape Crozier. They were astonished to find the shelter built forty-six years before still recognizable, with articles left by Wilson's party still inside it. On their major journey south the tractors performed wonderfully, although the soft surfaces and rarified air of the plateau taxed them to near their limit, and Hillary made unexpectedly fast progress in good weather conditions. The Ross sea party had laid all their depots by 20 December 1957, five days before Fuchs, after another harrowing journey from Shackleton to South Ice, was able to depart on his journey across the plateau.

It was clear that it would be some time before the two parties met and, although it had not been included in his programme, Hillary decided to make a dash for the Pole. There was no reason why he should not; other parties were carrying out the surveying work, and the idea was approved by the committees in New Zealand and London. It was only after this that direct radio contact between the two parties became possible and then Hillary rather incautiously suggested that, as it was getting late in the season, Fuchs should go no further than the Pole, and fly out leaving his vehicles there for a resumption of the journey the next summer. Fuchs replied, perhaps bluntly, that he intended to carry on. This was a private exchange, conducted, with no loss of temper, but somehow the media got to hear of it and magnified it into a major row between the two men. There can be no doubt that *Lo Scienziato* and *Lo sportivo neozelandese*, as Fuchs and Hillary were respectively described by an Italian writer, although different kinds of men, were certainly not enemies. Hillary and his party arrived at the US Amundsen-Scott South Pole Station on 4 January 1958, the first men to get to the spot by surface travel since Scott and his four companions.

Fuchs and his party left South Ice on Christmas Day with the vehicles – four Sno-cats, three Weasels and a Muskeg tractor – decked appropriately with flags and pennants. Once they were well on to the plateau they made good progress, averaging 50 kilometres (30 miles) a day. The routine was to make seismic soundings, in which timing the passage through the ice of shock waves from an explosion is used to give an estimate of its depth, and gravimetric determinations. These were later used to construct a profile of ice depth and elevation of the rock surface across the continent – a most valuable contribution. Vehicle maintenance had to be carried out in sub-zero temperatures routinely every 320 kilometres (200 miles), and of necessity at other times. Three Weasels, which had proved themselves better than tractors in soft snow, and a Muskeg had to be abandoned. The party reached the Pole, again flying every available flag and pennant, on 19 January 1958. A beaming Hillary was the first to greet Fuchs, whose first words were: 'It's damn good to see you, Ed.' The accompanying dog-teams were the first to reach the Pole since Amundsen's.

The trans-Antarctic journey was successfully completed on 2 March with the Sno-cats once again bedecked with flags and pennants to meet a cavalcade of vehicles from the McMurdo and Scott bases with a band which was loud, if nothing else. Fuchs had carried Captain Scott's watch, on a leather thong around his neck, all the way across. The crossing had taken ninety-nine days, one day less than Fuchs had thought necessary six years before, to do the 3473 kilometres (2158 miles). The achievement was crowned by the Otter from Shackleton flying across to Scott Base, aided, it has to be said, by a following wind which eked out its fuel, and thus becoming the first single-engined aircraft to fly across the continent via the South Pole.

It takes us well outside the Antarctic, but the staggering achievement of linking up transpolar expeditions, north and south, into a journey encircling the earth must be mentioned briefly. Such a circumnavigation was proposed by Charles de Brosses, an eighteenth-century French geographer, as desirable to establish the limits of temperature zones, but it had to wait until the idea was revived by Lady Twisleton-Wykeham-Fiennes, as something, it seems, to take her mind off the making of Irish stew, and until her husband, the authorities having ridiculed it, decided to prove that it could be done. To minimize political complications, the great circle through Greenwich was chosen, which meant starting the Antarctic leg near Sanae, the South African base, and taking an unexplored route to the Pole. A forward base was established in the Borga Massif, 240 kilometres (150 miles) south of Sanae, in which the party, with Lady Fiennes as radio operator, overwintered.

Ranulph Fiennes set out with two companions at the end of October 1980, each on a skidoo towing sledges, relying on depots laid by plane. Once a badly crevassed area had been passed, the main obstacles on the plateau were sastrugi – the skidoos could not ride over a vertical surface higher than 30 centimetres (1 foot), so a path had to be hacked through anything bigger – and the excruciating cold – the driver of a skidoo is exposed to the weather and does not get exercise to keep him warm. Nevertheless, the crossing was accomplished without serious accident; the Pole was reached on 15 December and Scott Base on Ross Island was reached sixty-seven days after the start of the journey. This had been done against the advice of many experts by men without previous Antarctic experience. That it was successful was due to the perfection of the techniques for travel and survival in polar regions which were available in 1980, careful planning, and the highly developed instinct for survival and determination to succeed of the people concerned. The Arctic crossing, over sea-ice, was even more testing, and one can only humbly admire the hardiness and courage which enabled Fiennes and his companions to bring the whole preposterous venture to a successful conclusion and to be the first men to have stood at both poles.[119]

Expeditions such as these contributed valuable scientific information about the Antarctic continent, but most of our knowledge has come from more humdrum systematic work which began in the International Geophysical Year of 1957-8. Between them, the twelve nations which participated in the Antarctic programme established thirty-nine stations on or close to the continent, and of these, nine were well inside it. The two most spectacular achievements were the setting up of the Amundsen-Scott Station by the United States at the Pole itself and of Sovetskaya by the USSR at the Pole of Inaccessibility, the spot furthest from approach by ship.

Amundsen-Scott Station was established entirely by air. First a refuelling and emergency base was set up at the foot of the Beardmore Glacier, between McMurdo Station and the Pole. Then twenty-four US Navy Seabees were landed at the Pole and Globemaster aircraft began dropping the materials and supplies required for the station. This was a prodigiously wasteful operation. Loads were dropped on parachutes which had a quick-release mechanism to detach them as soon as the snow surface was reached so as to avoid the package taking off across the plateau like a powered sledge in the high winds that prevailed. Unfortunately, these devices often functioned prematurely as the load left the plane and at other times parachutes failed to open with the result that many loads freefell and were smashed or buried so deeply that they could not be found. A tractor which severed its shroud lines as it fell landed like an exploding bomb and buried itself, shattered beyond repair, 10 metres (33 feet) down in the ice. But there was no other way that the station could have been put there. Planes which did land had great difficulty in taking off again in the thin air, even with lavish expenditure of JATO (Jet Assisted Take-Off) bottles.

In all, eighty-four flights dropped 760 tonnes of building materials, supplies, food and fuel, the station was completed in four months, the Seabees were flown out and the eighteen men who were to stay there flown in.[120] They had to face 186 days of darkness in which temperatures fell as low as $-74°C (-101°F)$. The Antarctic night produces derangements, both physiological, such as disruption of patterns of sleep, and psychological. The latter are compounded in a small community, living in cramped quarters with a minimum of contact with the external world, to give a psychologist's paradise. However, Richard Byrd was perhaps right when he summed up what men missed most in this situation with the single word 'temptation' and the intuitions and experience of a good leader sufficed to keep a wintering group on a level keel without psychiatric assistance. At Amundsen-Scott Station in 1957 problems were aggravated because there were two groups, the scientists and the naval support staff. The chief of the scientific staff was Paul Siple, who had been with Byrd on his first Antarctic expedition; Lieutenant John Tuck led the naval team. Inevitably there was friction, but thanks to full programmes of work for both groups and good sense from the two leaders winter passed in reasonable harmony. Celebrations are great morale boosters on Antarctic bases and 22 June, Midwinter Day, the day when the sun begins to return, is a traditional occasion for a holiday and party. At Amundsen-Scott there were paper decorations, balloons, turkey and toasts in champagne among which was one from Siple: 'To Byrd, and to Scott, Amundsen and all those who made our presence here possible – To Antarctica'. Time zones and even dates are confusing in this part of the world and at Shackleton celebrations had been held the previous day. There was a cocktail party, fireworks, again a turkey dinner, crackers and presents, and finally a buffet supper with mustard and cress grown on the premises.

Politically and juridically, Amundsen-Scott Station is a nightmare – an installation paid for by a nation which does not recognize territorial claims in the Antarctic sitting in an area where six other nations assert sovereign rights. Scientifically, there is much to be said for it – it is, for example, the only place where the face of the sun can be observed continuously over twenty-four hours in December. Amundsen-Scott Station has been manned permanently since 1957.

The setting up of a station at the Pole of Inaccessibility was even more difficult than it was at the South Pole itself. The Soviets decided to do it by

The Lemaire Channel (water-colour)

means of an over-snow tractor train – wisely, as it turned out, because their first attempt failed when they ran into conditions which were impossible for tractors and which would have been disastrous for aircraft. Whereas over most of the continent the wind packs the snow sufficiently for it to bear tracked vehicles, in this relatively calm heartland the snow was fluffy and deep. For the following season, in 1958, tractors were built with wider treads and special air compressors to give more power to the engines in the rarified air on the plateau. A caravan of ten tractors each with two heavy sledges in tow set out from Mirny, the USSR station on the Indian Ocean sector of the coast, after speeches and firing of rockets. When it reached Komsomolskaya, 450 nautical miles inland, it divided, one party going to Vostok, a station newly established at the South Geomagnetic Pole, and the other to the Pole of Inaccessibility. The latter route took them up to more than 3600 metres (11,800 feet), at which height even the supercharged engines faltered, and into snow in which the tractors with their 120-tonne burden sometimes sank to a depth of 1.5 metres (5 feet). Even the robust and hardened Soviets themselves were affected by the altitude and 350 nautical miles short of their destination their leader Vitali K. Babarykin decided enough was enough. Scientifically, there was no point in carrying on as one spot was as good as another in this hostile and featureless wilderness.

The station was built and five men left to winter. They had a grim time, suffering headaches and shortness of breath as well as temperatures of around $-59°C$ ($-74°F$) to start with and later falling to below $-70°C$ ($-94°F$). Electrically heated clothes had to be used for outdoor work. Water dropped on ice outdoors danced as on a hot stove, freezing immediately into pearl-like droplets, and paraffin congealed to something resembling wet snow. Nevertheless, only 1000 metres (3300 feet) overhead was relatively warm air which had streamed down to Antarctica from hotter climes. In spring fresh food was air-dropped to Sovetskaya and later a sortie was made which did reach the Pole of Inaccessibility itself. Two weeks was spent in making measurements; it was found that the ice was about 2900 metres (9500 feet) thick over rock only some 800 metres above sea level. The annual snow fall was estimated as equivalent to 1 centimetre ($\frac{1}{2}$ inch) of water – about the same precipitation as falls on the Sahara. Sovetskaya has not been maintained on a permanent basis.[121]

By the end of the International Geophysical Year the general form of the Antarctic continent was clear. The great chain of the Transantarctic Mountains extends in a shallow 'S'-shape, running along the west coast of the huge embayment of the Ross Sea and the east coast of the equally enormous Weddell Sea, and dividing the continent into Lesser or West Antarctica, which includes the Peninsula, and Greater or East Antarctica. Over all, covering everything except 1 per cent, is ice, rising in a dome to over 4000 metres (13,100 feet) above sea level and spreading out over the edges of the land as shelves. The questions which immediately arise are how deep is this ice? What is underneath it – a single land mass, two land masses, or several archipelagos? And most important, how much ice is there? The answer to this last question has tremendous implications for world meteorology, oceanography and geological history.

Seismic sounding, as done on the Trans-Antarctic Expedition, is a slow business, using cumbersome equipment, and giving only a few widely-spaced results, some of which may be difficult to interpret. However, this technique did show that the ice is of considerable thickness in most places and that there is a deep trench between Greater and Lesser Antarctica, so that they evidently are separate masses of land. Radio echo sounding, which was developed in the 1960s by S. Evans and G. de L. Robin of the Scott Polar Research Institute in Cambridge and later by the Technical University of Denmark, is a much more satisfactory method. It works on much the same principle as the sonic echo-sounder used at sea, with high-frequency pulsed radar directed downwards from an aircraft. Echos are reflected back from both ice-sheet surface and bedrock and the times taken give estimates both of ice thickness and vertical distance of the ice surface below the plane. The US Antarctic Research Programme provided air facilities for trying the technique in Antarctica and since then it has been widely used by scientists from many nations and from satellites as well as aircraft so that now more than half of the continent has been sounded on a 50–100-kilometre (31–62 mile) grid on flights adding up to 500,000 kilometres (300,000 miles).

The three-dimensional picture which has emerged shows that the tremendous weight of ice, 27,000 million million tonnes of it, has pressed the land surface down below sea-level over large areas.[122] The thickest ice is, surprisingly, not far away from the coast in Adélie Land, where a huge depression, some 2000 metres (6600 feet) or more below sea-level deep, contains a thickness of 4750 metres (15,580 feet) of ice. The lowest point of the continent, 2538 metres (8327 feet) below sea-level, is in a trench situated in West Antarctica. There are mountains concealed beneath the ice and some of the thinnest ice is near Sovetskaya, where one might expect it to be the thickest, where the Gamburtsev Mountains, invisible at the surface, rise to 2750 metres (9020 feet) above sea-level. In places there are large lakes under the ice, which is thick enough to provide insulation from the cold and allow the temperature to get up to a level at which the ice melts under pressure. It seems unlikely that there can be anything living in these lakes, but bacteria have been found in even more unpromising habitats.

The volume of all this ice is estimated to be 30 million cubic kilometres (7.2 million cubic miles) – equivalent to about ten times as much water as there is in the Mediterranean or a tenth of that in the Indian Ocean. If it were to melt, the sea-level would rise by 60 metres (200 feet) – submerging Nelson on his column in Trafalgar Square, London, and inundating large areas of densely populated land throughout the world. The stability of the ice-sheet is literally of vital concern to humanity.

As mentioned already, ice behaves as a viscous plastic material and flows outwards from the centre of the continent under its own weight. As a result, its surface tends to a parabolic profile although this may be distorted by the irregular terrain beneath it. The central regions are flat, with gradients around 1 : 1000, and the flow is extremely slow. Towards the edge, slopes are steeper and rates of flow higher. The ice is also thinner and features of the buried rock surface may be seen, somewhat blurred, in the ice surface from plane or satellite. Where channelled into glaciers, velocities are greater and the ice becomes crevassed and broken into ice-falls. Fast-flowing zones within the ice-sheet itself may develop and these are known as ice-streams. Loss from the ice-cap in the form of icebergs is difficult to estimate but may be about 2.3 million million tonnes each year. The annual accumulation of snow over Antarctica is thought to be some 2 million million tonnes. These figures suggest that the ice-cap is in balance or contracting slightly but other methods of calculation indicate that it is increasing. Ice-streams may stop for no very obvious reason and, disquietingly, sudden surges may occur. Since the fate of the Antarctic ice is of such dire consequence for us it would be good to know exactly what is happening and much research effort is being devoted to finding out.[123]

One unexpected and convenient property of the ice-cap is that it is the perfect collecting device for meteorites. Elsewhere these are usually difficult to find and when found are contaminated with terrestrial material. Those falling on the ice-sheet are not only preserved in pristine condition but, in places where ice is dammed up behind mountain ranges and the surface is gradually worn away by wind and sublimation, are actually collected together from a large catchment area by ice movements. Such a hoard was found by chance by Japanese scientists in 1969 and since then more than 6000 meteorite fragments have come to light in Antarctica, increasing the world total by about a quarter. These meteorites are especially valuable to cosmologists not only because of their good condition but because they probably give a better cross-section of the different sorts of material which fall on us from outer space, than do collections from elsewhere.[123]

The ice of Antarctica yields exceptionally pure water on melting, purer than analytical quality distilled water, and it is therefore ironic that one of its main interests should lie in its impurities. As snow falls, it brings with it dusts and aerosols from the air – desert dust, sea salts, volcanic ash, industrial pollutants and cosmic dust – and these are incorporated, together with bubbles of air, in the ice as it is laid down. These samples of air and what was in it are preserved indefinitely, without biological or chemical alteration, in strict chronological order – a marvellous historical record. By meticulous analysis of samples from cores of Antarctic ice, taken, of course, under conditions of surgical cleanliness and transported, still frozen, to laboratories in the northern hemisphere where they can be handled without contamination, much can be learnt of what went on in the world as far back as 150,000 years ago. For example, analyses can be made of the carbon dioxide content of trapped air to determine the fluctuations in the concentration of this gas in the atmosphere in the past, a matter of great interest in connection with the 'greenhouse effect'. These show that during the last glacial maximum, 20,000 years ago, the concentration was as low as 0.020 per cent. By AD 1750 it had risen to 0.028 per cent and from then on it has risen at an ever-increasing rate to reach about 0.034 per cent at present.

Conviction that this sort of increase is going to have effects on climate is strengthened by another kind of analysis, on the water itself, which gives a measure of temperatures in the past. The oxygen in water, H_2O, is mostly the isotope of atomic weight 16, ^{16}O, but a small proportion is ^{18}O. Being heavier, $H_2^{18}O$ evaporates slightly less readily than does $H_2^{16}O$, and the ratio between the two forms in water vapour depends on the temperature at which evaporation took place. So, by measuring the ratio of $^{16}O : ^{18}O$ in the ice, one has an index of average temperatures at the time the water originally evaporated from the ocean. Analysis from a core 2000 metres (6600 feet) long obtained at the USSR Vostok Station shows the climate oscillating between warm and cold over the past 150,000 years with present temperatures at a high level after recovery from the last ice age. There is a striking – one would say chilling were it not inappropriate in the context – correlation between carbon dioxide concentrations and the isotope ratio. These ice-core results strongly suggest that accumulating carbon dioxide in the atmosphere will produce global warming with all its possibly catastrophic consequences for mankind. Another measure of pollution is given by analyses for lead. Concentrations in Antarctic ice have increased some forty-fold in the last few thousand years but no recent increase is evident although Greenland ice shows a four-fold greater concentration now than fifty years ago. Evidently the lead which is poured into the atmosphere from motor exhausts takes a little time to work its way down to the southern hemisphere. An Antarctic ice-core is one of the best yard-sticks we have for assessing the long-term effects of man's activities on the world environment.[122]

The structure of the rocky foundation underlying the ice has already been touched on in describing the Peninsula. Greater Antarctica is the easily-recognized key-stone of the super-continent Gondwanaland and consists of a 'shield' of ancient granite and metamorphosed rocks which has probably been more or less stable for the last 360 million years. Along one edge the

Transantarctic Mountains seem to have been uplifted by tectonic activity along the boundary between Greater and Lesser Antarctica. The only remnant of this activity today is seen in the volcano Mount Erebus. In the Transantarctic range the ancient folded sediments are overlain by a flat-lying sequence of unaltered sediments, mostly sandstones and poor in fossils with extensive but poor-quality coalfields on top, known as the Beacon Group. These yellow, or buff, horizontal strata, contrasting with intrusive sills of dark dolerite, contribute the distinctive banded element in the scenery of the Transantarctic Mountains. Lesser Antarctica seems to be made up of several continental fragments which have moved relative to each other and, as we have seen, the Peninsula is still something of a geological enigma.

A remarkable feature of the continent today is its apparent freedom from earthquakes, such small local tremors as are recorded by seismographs being attributable to calving of icebergs. It may be that the vast plaster of ice lying over the rock crust inhibits earthquakes, or it may be that the continent's situation on the axis of spin of the earth gives it some special stability. Another point of interest in Antarctica for geologists, of course, is that here they can see in action the glacial processes which shaped much of our own northern landscapes.[122]

Among the few areas in Antarctica where the geologist can actually see extensive areas of the rocks he wants to study, are the oases or dry valleys, places which are perennially free from ice and snow. The first of these areas, unique to Antarctica, was discovered by Scott, in company with seamen Evans and Lashly, in December 1903, on their way back from a sledging expedition in the mountains of Victoria Land. They descended from the Ferrar Glacier into a strange valley:

> ...a very wonderful place. We have seen today all the indications of colossal ice action and considerable water action, and yet neither of these agents is now at work. It is worthy of record, too, that we have seen no living thing, not even a moss or lichen; all that we did find, far inland among the moraine heaps, was the skeleton of a Weddell seal, and how that came there is beyond guessing. It is certainly a valley of the dead; even the great glacier which once pushed through it has withered away.[124]

He and his companions revelled in the comparative warmth and found a frozen lake and curiously shaped boulders. Scott later named this valley after Griffith Taylor, who carried out the first thorough survey of it on the 1910–13 expedition.

Similar snow-free areas have since been found all around Antarctica: by the British Graham Land Expedition on Alexander Island in 1936, in the Vestfold Hills on the Ingrid Christensen Coast by Klarius Mikkelsen in 1935, and the Bunger Oasis on the border between Queen Mary Land and

196

Wilkes Land by the US Operation Highjump in 1947. The term 'oasis', first used in a throw-away comment by Alfred Stephenson when he discovered the one on Alexander Island, is not appropriate, for these are not oases but deserts as dry as the Sahara, and led to a preposterous press release about an Antarctic Shangri-la, green with vegetation, when the Operation Highjump discovery was announced. Various reasons for absence of snow and ice have been put forward – radioactivity, subterranean coal fires and volcanic activity – but the explanation is the less exotic one that the rate of loss of snow and ice by ablation exceeds the rate of input. The first requirement must be that the local topography is such that flow of ice is diverted away from the area. Once bare patches persist, the increased absorption of heat from the sun makes the local climate warmer and drier.

The first major project in one of these geological paradises was the Dry Valley Drilling Project which began in 1971 and was carried out jointly by the United States, New Zealand and Japan. Drilling is an expensive business and drill rigs are cumbersome, but the dry valleys of Victoria Land are within helicopter range of McMurdo Station. A preliminary aeromagnetic survey provided basic information about the area and trial drilling was first carried out near McMurdo. This was the first rock drilling done on the continent but it was remarkably successful, with a total of 2 kilometres (1.2 miles) of core obtained from fifteen holes, providing much information about the geological history over the last 10 million years of this part of Antarctica.

For the layman, the most dramatic manifestation of the geological processes going on in the dry valleys is seen in the strange and beautiful shapes of the boulders. The fierce winds loaded with abrasive sand have cut and polished rocks with facets and flutings to give objects, known as 'ventefacts', some of which might steal the show at any exhibition of sculpture. Another type of erosion occurs in coarsely crystalline rocks such as granite, when dehydrated salts in interstices between crystals take up water and expand, breaking off particles. This process goes on more rapidly on protected surfaces which thereby tend to become concave and boulders are eventually hollowed out or pierced by holes. Comparison with the works of Henry Moore is irresistible. These natural sculptures are set, Japanese fashion, in sand, the product of their own decay. They, and the dry valleys themselves, are well portrayed in the photographs of Eliot Porter.[125] The uncanny atmosphere is enhanced by utter silence.

Streams and lakes are to be found in the dry valleys but are of peculiar kinds. The Onyx River in the Wright Valley is one of the few watercourses in Antarctica that can be dignified by the title 'river', although it exists very much on a stop-go basis as temperatures oscillate around freezing point. It has its origin in melt-water from the Wright Glacier and flows 40 kilometres (25 miles) towards the head of the valley where it drains into Lake Vanda.

This lake, which is named after a dog called Vanda, has no outflow and is permanently ice-covered. Immediately under the ice its waters are as cold and pure as any lake waters in the world, but, amazingly, the bottom water, which is saline, has a temperature of 25°C (77°F), 46°C (83°F) above the mean temperature of the region. The first suggestion was that this must be caused by hot spring activity but it is now generally accepted that Lake Vanda is a natural solar heating device. The candle ice (see page 144) at its surface provides light-pipes to exceptionally clear water below, allowing solar radiation to penetrate deeply. There it heats the saline water which, because of its high density, is prevented from mixing with the water above. The ice cover, of course, helps by protecting the water from mixing by wind. There is life in the form of algae, bacteria and protozoa but, the lake being almost sealed off from the outer world except for input of solar energy, the organisms live by recycling nutrients between them – taking in each other's washing. New Zealand maintains a base on the shore of Lake Vanda.

Another remarkable water body in the Wright Valley is Don Juan Pond, the oily-looking shallow waters of which are dotted with ventefacts. The water is a nearly saturated solution of calcium chloride so it never freezes even at temperatures as low as −51°C (−60°F). Japanese workers have discovered in it a mineral new to science, crystals of a hydrated form of calcium chloride given the name of 'antarcticite', which liquify unless kept refrigerated. That Don Juan Pond accumulates calcium chloride must reflect the vagaries of drainage off an area in which different types of mineral are decomposing. The saline bottom waters of Lake Vanda probably arose by concentration through evaporation followed by fresh water flowing on top when wetter conditions returned.[126]

Scott was not right in dismissing dry valleys as lifeless, but he can be excused because the organisms are far from obvious, being microbes.

Bacteria, microscopic algae, and, to a lesser extent, yeasts and protozoa are to be found in the mineral debris – one can scarcely call it soil – on the floors of the valleys. In the very driest parts even these are absent, but as conditions ameliorate by becoming only slightly moister, the micro-organisms become reasonably abundant. One point of interest about them is that they represent a microbial community which exists without the complications caused by large animals and plants or by much invasion by airborne microbes from elsewhere. This is a condition that has to be carefully guarded if it is to remain useful for scientific study and one dry valley, Barwick Valley, is protected rigorously from visits to conserve its microbial community. Another feature is that the algae and lichens are mainly 'endolithic', that is, they grow within rock in the interstices between crystals. This is also the habit of algae growing in hot deserts. It seems that in these two otherwise different situations it affords protection from extreme desiccation and strong light.

Any animal that wanders into a dry valley is doomed to die and in the extreme cold and dryness its body will be mummified and perhaps preserved for several thousand years. That is clear but what remains a mystery is why so many seals and penguins should have found their way up to the dry valleys of Victoria Land, some 80 kilometres (50 miles) from the sea.

The dry valleys of Antarctica give the nearest approach that we have on earth to the conditions we believe to prevail on the surface of Mars. The terrain is no doubt similar and the life, if any, on Mars would be expected to be of the same general forms as that in the dry valleys, although the virtual absence of free oxygen would make vital processes somewhat different. The dry valleys have consequently been used by space scientists as testing grounds for vehicles designed to land on and sample planetary surfaces.[107]

Tabular iceberg,
Weddell Sea
(water-colour)

Taking possession, Possession Island, 11 January 1841. Watercolour by J. E. Davis. (Courtesy of the Scott Polar Research Institute)

Chapter Ten

Hope out of Antarctica?

W HAT IS THE GOOD of all this effort in Antarctica? It is the most remote and hostile part of the globe, getting there is still difficult, dangerous and expensive, and when one is there one finds little but vast expanses of icy desert. To answer grandly, as did the climbers of Everest, 'because it is there', is really not adequate.

The lure of valuable material resources has often been used to attract support, but still, after more than 200 years of exploration, this wealth has nearly all proved to be unsustainable or illusory. The El Dorado placed in Terra Australis Incognita was shown to be a figment by Cook; a few made huge profits from sealing or whaling in the Southern Ocean but quickly reduced the goose to a state in which she could no longer lay golden eggs; Ernest Shackleton was full of schemes for making his fortune but never did.

Oil, minerals and krill are now considered as possible exploitable resources. Seismic traverses, airborne radio echo-sounding and sea-bed drilling, even if carried out with no immediate commercial motive, yield results which oil companies examine with interest. Oil itself has not yet been found in the Antarctic but natural gas, an indicator of its possible presence, has been detected and the geological structures likely to hold oil are there. Oil is perhaps present in quantity but the problems of tapping it are formidable.[128] On land, the moving ice-sheet, and at sea, the great depth of the continental shelf, sea-ice and gigantic icebergs, make the installation and operation of wells, if not impossible, then extremely hazardous and expensive. Oil spills in Antarctica would be particularly damaging since low temperatures would slow down their dissipation by volatilization, dispersion, and breakdown by bacteria. The precautions on which conservationists would rightly insist might by themselves be prohibitive.

The likelihood of finding valuable and economically workable mineral deposits, discussed in Chapter Seven (see page 156), seems low. Even a valuable mineral available in the Antarctic in prodigous quantities in exceptionally pure form and conveniently packaged for towing away in floating pieces cannot be got to where it is needed before it melts (see page 114). The harvesting of krill, also mentioned earlier (see page 104), is doubtfully viable, unless subsidized, being on the one hand a difficult material to process for human food and on the other too expensive to use for animal feed. There is also the problem in the present state of knowledge of knowing how much may be taken without doing serious damage to the marine ecosystem of the Antarctic.[128] It may be that some unexpected valuable resource awaits discovery but, as things are, it seems that explorers and scientists might be accused of having oversold the natural resources of the Antarctic. As often happens, however, a venture into the unknown has produced results of a totally unexpected nature which are perhaps more valuable than those originally envisaged.

In the old days, of course, a claim to sovereignty in the Antarctic was more of a precautionary measure in case there was anything of value there, rather than an assertion of ownership of known resources. There were other considerations too – geopolitics, strategy, national prestige – but, one feels, taking possession was often little more than a pleasant ritual to encourage the troops. Cook, Smith, Biscoe and Ross, whenever they landed, planted the Union Jack, fired a volley of shots, and proclaimed the land as a possession of the Crown for the benefit of perplexed penguins. The glory of their country was a prime motive for these explorers, as we have already seen in quotations from members of the d'Urville and Ross expeditions given in Chapter One (see page 32). To these may be added one from Wilkes, who, after indulging in his autobiography in a diatribe about the imbecility and incompetence of the administration which had dispatched him south, went on:

> But I had the cause of my Country at heart, and the disgrace which had attended the getting up of the Expedition and its failure and folly, as well as the honest expectations of the whole country, made me consider the whole in another light. I had made up my mind the Expedition Should Not fail in my hands and believed I could carry it out to a successful issue.[129]

Despite the rivalries between the American, British and French expeditions in the mid-nineteenth century, the decencies were preserved and civilities exchanged although there was no co-operation or rationalization of their

Grytviken whaling station (oil)

overlapping aims. The Australians welcomed all three expeditions warmly and gave them generous help, although only for the British was a specially written play put on to celebrate their achievements.

By the turn of the century there was a limited amount of co-operation and joint planning at the international level, but at the same time intense rivalry, which expressed itself in the race for the Pole between Amundsen and Scott. Amundsen was single-minded in his determination to win for Norway and himself the glory of being first at the South Pole but, although he concealed this intention with somewhat unworthy skill until the latest possible moment, he was scrupulous in not using the route pioneered by Scott and Shackleton. In the last stages of the journey anxiety lest Scott should have forestalled him was intense. At the Pole he left a note for Scott, wishing him well and asking him to convey a letter reporting his success to King Haakon.[130] This was probably no more than sensible precaution against not surviving the return journey, but to someone in Scott's state of mind it seemed to have a flavour of insult to 'our poor slighted Union Jack'. Scott, of course, had had no idea of the Norwegians' progress towards the Pole and, until he got there, had a personal rivalry with Shackleton foremost in his mind, matching each day's march against the corresponding one of his one-time sledging companion.[131]

Before Amundsen's intentions to go to the South Pole were known Scott had taken on, as ski expert, a young Norwegian, Tryggve Gran, who himself had been planning an Antarctic expedition. Gran fitted in well and the news of competition from his compatriot, although it strained his loyalties, does not seem to have altered the friendship for him felt in Scott's party. Scott himself, inclined to be short-tempered anyway, was for a time unreasonably rough with him. This phase passed, however; Scott admitted that he had misjudged him and Gran might well have been included in the polar journey but for Amundsen's challenge. On his side, Gran remained a devoted admirer of Scott to the end of his long life. He was in the party which discovered the tent on the Barrier with the bodies of Scott and his two companions. There was deep emotion on both sides when Tom Crean, a seaman, passed on to him the news that Scott's diary recorded the finding of the Norwegian flag at the Pole and extended his hand in congratulation. It was Gran's skis which were used to make the cross surmounting the cairn over the bodies and Gran used Scott's skis on the journey back to Cape Evans, so they at any rate would 'complete the 3,000 km trail'.[132]

Those not directly involved were less generous; Kathleen Scott's dislike of Amundsen is understandable but the conventional British opinion, expressed by Scott's patron, Sir Clements Markham, in the descriptions 'interloper' and 'gad-fly', was petty and congratulations were grudging. Alone among the British Antarctic establishment Shackleton recognized the magnitude of the achievement, although Amundsen's lectures were well received by the general public. In Norway there was unease at having antagonized a powerful neighbour. Amundsen himself came to feel that he had some responsibility for Scott's death. There was a spare tin of paraffin which he might have left for Scott to find at the Pole and this, perhaps, might have made all the difference. In 1928 Amundsen perished in an attempt to fly to the rescue of the Italian Umberto Nobile, who tried unsuccessfully to reach the North Pole by airship.[133]

Nevertheless, at this time there was no particular political significance in Antarctica. There had been scarcely a ripple when in 1908 the British government issued Letters Patent asserting sovereignty over a substantial wedge of Antarctica including the South Orkneys, South Shetlands and the Peninsula. In origin this was an act to conserve whales rather than imperialistic expansion, but by 1920 the government had decided secretly to pursue a policy aimed at gradual acquisition, for imperialistic and strategic reasons, of the entire continent. Another Order in Council establishing the Ross Dependency to be administered by New Zealand followed in 1923, then in the following year the French inserted a slim but effective spanner in the works by claiming the Adélie Land sector in spite of the fact that no Frenchman had yet set foot on its mainland. There was agitation from the intensely patriotic Australian Antarctic veteran, Sir Douglas Mawson, that this should be opposed, but the British government thought it wiser to accept the situation. Australia eventually and somewhat reluctantly proclaimed sovereignty over the sector between 40°E and 160°E with the exception of the sliver of Adélie Land.

In 1928 Byrd had begun his series of expeditions and in 1935 Ellsworth flew over the continent, both of them depositing claims on behalf of the USA at strategic spots. In spite of pressure from these explorers, the US government advanced no claims and maintained an equivocal attitude, sticking on the whole to the principle that a claim could only be valid if based on 'effective occupation' and irritating the British government by ignoring its assertions of sovereignty. By 1939 the Norwegians, whose whalers had carried out extensive explorations in the Atlantic sector, felt it necessary to make a claim in view of planes, overflying this region from the Schwabenland expedition under the personal patronage of Reichsmarschall Hermann Göring, which had scattered spear-like markers carrying the swastika. Britain's grand design was thus looking the worse for wear when the Second World War broke out and Antarctica became of strategic importance in reality.[134]

The lonely seas and islands of the Southern Ocean were just the place for raiders to lurk. The U-boat *Pinguin*, based on Kerguelen, captured in one fell swoop an entire Norwegian whaling fleet as it lay at anchor off Queen Maud

Land. After it had been found and sunk by HMS *Cornwall* in May 1941, its sister submarines *Komet* and *Atlantis* continued to harass Allied shipping. In 1940 Chile, emulating Norway, made a claim in the Peninsula sector which overlapped with the Falkland Islands Dependencies. Britain was too much preoccupied with other things to bother much about this but when Argentina, which had made desultory claims to Antarctic territories in 1925 and 1937, also made a definite and substantial claim in this sector in 1943, it was a different matter. It would not do to have a power which favoured Germany controlling the southern side of the Drake Passage. This was the reason for the dispatch of the secret naval expedition, code-named Operation Tabarin, which after the war took on a scientific character and became the Falkland Islands Dependencies Survey.

Argentina continued to maintain her claim and for a decade or so there was friction which largely took the form of ritual exchange of protest notes and removal of the other side's official marks and notices. A more serious thing was when the Argentinians built a block-house in the middle of the Fids' football pitch on Deception Island. That was blown up after a police-man from the Falkland Islands was brought in to remove the occupants, who went quietly. Shots were fired by the Argentinians when the British landed to re-establish their base at Hope Bay on the tip of the Peninsula but this was resolved by the Governor of the Falkland Islands sailing for Hope Bay, with the utmost dispatch before the Colonial Office could stop him, in HMS *Burghead Bay*.[83]

As well as these comic-opera episodes, the opening scenes of a potential tragedy were being played. Immediately after the war, the United States had reasserted its interest with the massive Operation Highjump, which was frankly military and with a minimum of science. This was looked at askance by Argentina and Chile as well as Australia, New Zealand and the United Kingdom and possibly as a reassurance the US took the diplomatic initiative in 1948 by suggesting that Antarctica should be put under international trusteeship. The Soviets, who so far had shown no interest in the Antarctic and who were not included in this invitation, then fired a warning shot over the US bows in a diplomatic note to the nations negotiating the condominium, stating that they would refuse to recognize as lawful any decisions about a regime for Antarctica taken without their participation. This was at the height of the cold war and things began to look black.[135]

The miracle which happened then began in April 1950 in after-dinner conviviality in the Maryland home of an American scientist, James van Allen, who was entertaining a British guest, Sydney Chapman. Those present were all interested in the physics of the upper atmosphere and the idea came up that the best thing to further their science would be another international polar year, the last one, in 1932–3, having been not too successful

206

mainly because of the great depression, and, moreover, techniques had advanced enormously since then. The proposal was put to the International Council of Scientific Unions, which approved the idea but thought that the scope should be broadened into an International Geophysical Year (IGY) to run in the years 1957 and 1958. Work in the Antarctic was to be a main part of the programme. By May 1954, the deadline for submission of detailed projects, scientists of over twenty nations had agreed to participate and the US had set an example with government approval and massive financial support. Nothing had been heard from the USSR but, after the death of Stalin in 1953, Soviet scientists had been joining more freely in international discussions and in October 1954 it became known that they would participate in IGY. Nine months later there was a dramatic announcement that they would be sending an expedition to the Antarctic. The meetings planning the Antarctic work had some critical moments but most fortunately the chairman, a Frenchman, Colonel Georges Laclavère, was quietly firm in insisting that no political considerations should be allowed to intrude on the science. Co-operation was ensured from the moment that the US agreed that there should be a Soviet scientist at the Weather Centre at Little America and in return Moscow offered a place at its main base to an American. The IGY was a resounding success in the estimation of scientists and tremendously impressive for the non-scientific world. For Antarctic research, it was the beginning of a new era. Twelve nations joined in the Antarctic work of IGY, the number of stations increased from twenty to forty-eight and the wintering population rose from 179 to 912, with a summer population of as much as 5000.[136]

If the scientific results were gratifying, the political outcome was momentous. Nations, some of diametrically opposed ideologies and some with conflicting territorial claims in Antarctica, had worked together amicably and constructively. The USSR had, with the approval of the other nations, established itself on the continent and when it became evident that it was there to stay, the US had no option but to maintain its presence in Antarctica too. With the object of regularizing the situation, the US government circulated a note to the eleven other nations with Antarctic interests proposing a treaty that would set the continent aside for scientific activities. It seemed that the moratorium on political argument that had prevailed during the IGY should be continued. Britain, having failed in its attempt to get Argentina to agree to having the dispute between them settled by the International Court of Justice, put its weight behind this idea of internationalization. Meetings were held in great secrecy and there was much behind-the-scenes diplomacy. For a time the Soviets were awkward, maintaining that these were nothing more than talks about talks, then patience and conciliation paid off and suddenly they agreed that a draft treaty should be drawn up. Thus the Antarctic

Treaty came into force in June 1961. It was a triumph for the perspicacity of the diplomats who had seen the accord created by science as a means of bypassing the log-jam of conflicting claims to sovereignty, but it was also a matter of luck that the negotiations had been concluded during a brief easing in east-west tension – the U-2 spy plane affair brought about the collapse of the 1960 summit conference shortly after the Treaty was signed.[137]

Not the least of the Antarctic Treaty's several unique features is that its text has had a wider circulation among the general public than any other similar document. It has been reproduced in numerous popular and scientific books about Antarctica and has even appeared in the notes accompanying a gramophone record.[138] It need not be given yet again in this book, brief and to the point though it is. The essence is that Antarctica, defined as the area south of 60°S, should be used exclusively for peaceful purposes, any sort of military manoeuvre or testing of weapons being prohibited, although military personnel or equipment may be used in scientific research. Besides freedom to carry out research, co-operation and exchange of results between nations are to be promoted. Claims to territorial rights in Antarctica are not to be renounced but put in cold storage; no new claims can be made or grounds for new claims established so long as the Treaty is in force (this particular Article has been described as 'contrived ambiguity'). Each nation subscribing to the Treaty has the right to inspect the installations and work of the others. There is to be no disposal of radioactive waste and measures must be taken to conserve the living resources of Antarctica. The Treaty can only be modified or amended by unanimous agreement of the signatories. The common supposition that the Treaty is for a period of thirty years only, and therefore ends in 1991, is incorrect. This is only a date set for a review of the operation of the Treaty should any of the participating nations request it. Otherwise the Treaty remains in force indefinitely.[139]

The political innovation in this Treaty was to concentrate on positive action which everyone could agree should be taken and to set aside matters, such as sovereignty, on which agreement was not possible. The power of an Antarctic Treaty state lies in refusing to take part in a consensus, but it cannot alter a situation in its favour by doing this, change only being possible if all parties agree to it. A further feature distinguishing the Treaty is that, so far, it has no permanent headquarters or secretariat, its consultative meetings taking place in turn in the different participating countries. So there is a minimum of bureaucracy. The advice and detailed work on which the operation of the Treaty depends is carried out by a body with which it has no official connection, the Scientific Committee for Antarctic Research (SCAR), set up by the International Council of Scientific Unions, a non-governmental body run by scientists.[140] These arrangements have so far preserved the peace in Antarctica; even when two participating nations,

Argentina and the United Kingdom, went to war, the 60°S boundary was scrupulously observed and conflict did not extend into the Treaty area. Indeed, scientists from the two countries encountered amicably in Hobart, Tasmania, while the war was on, to discuss the conservation of living resources in the Antarctic. This was something of a return to the more civilized habits of the early nineteenth century when it was possible for Sir Humphrey Davy to be an honoured guest in France at the height of the Napoleonic Wars.

Beyond this, the Treaty has been flexible enough to allow expansions in scope and in the number of participating nations. To join the 'club', a nation has to show a substantial commitment to Antarctic research and it is greatly to the credit of the established members that they have been ready to pass on their experience to newcomers. This has certainly helped to preserve the sense of unity and common purpose on which the success of the Treaty so largely depends. By 1988, the number of participating nations had risen to eighteen. While SCAR has been responsible for organizing research programmes at the international level, the Treaty organization has carried through two major pieces of legislation, one on the conservation of Antarctic marine living resources, signed in 1980,[141] and the other on regulation of mineral exploitation, agreed in 1988.[142] It remains to be seen how effective these conventions will be – discovery of a really valuable mineral resource will be the supreme test of the strength of the Treaty – but they are unique and greatly encouraging in that they have been drawn up before, and not after, serious damage to the environment has occurred.

The Antarctic Treaty is thus something new and hopeful in international politics. In formulating it, politicians have, probably quite inadvertently, allowed science to become a political force in this limited area and the standard of discourse between nations has thereby been raised to a worthy level. It should provide a model for further improvements in the machinery of world politics and, indeed, it has already done so for the Outer Space and Seabed Treaties. Here are grounds for optimism. Nevertheless, the Treaty has its critics and there are weaknesses that may destroy the accord that it has so far maintained.

The Antarctic Treaty organization is regarded as an exclusive club by many nations which do not belong to it and these are resentful of the assumption by its members of the right to legislate for a large piece of the earth's surface over which these members arguably do not have sovereign rights.[143] Although the Treaty states that its intention is to further the objects of the United Nations, it is not itself a product of the United Nations and there is a large body of non-Treaty states which holds that this is wrong. These argue that Antarctica should be part of the common heritage of mankind and in recent years have regularly brought the 'Question of Antarctica'

Laws Glacier, Signy Island (water-colour)

before the United Nations with the object of having Antarctica brought under United Nations control. Actually, the concept of a 'common heritage of mankind' is not applicable to Antarctica under international law, and one may suspect those who try to insist that it is of wishing to participate in a hypothetical share-out of resources without having themselves put any effort into exploration and research. The advocates of the common heritage view seem to require the nations which discovered Antarctica to renounce the national heritages of which they have every justification to feel proud.

The strength of the Antarctic Treaty is that action taken under its aegis has to be agreed unanimously by a small group of representatives of those who have direct experience of Antarctic conditions. A transfer to United Nations jurisdiction would presumably mean that decisions would be taken by a large body with a majority of members with no expert knowledge of the Antarctic but preoccupied with political issues or irresponsible exploitation of resources. A better recipe for disaster could scarcely be found. Fortunately, given that the three major Antarctic powers have the power of veto in the United Nations, it does not seem that any drastic revision of the Treaty is likely from this quarter. The strength of the non-Treaty faction was greatly reduced when India, one of its most powerful members, decided to under-take Antarctic research and subscribe to the Treaty. In the course of time, no doubt, the dominant issue of sovereignty will die away, as it already has done in the consciousness of scientists. A more serious immediate threat arises from the existence of South Africa as a Consultative Party. This gives offence to many outside the Treaty, but the tradition of not allowing politi-cal considerations to intrude into Antarctic affairs has meant that, so far, it has not caused difficulties within the Treaty organization. If it did, it would be impossible to do anything about it without disrupting the Treaty; the consensus rule in the Treaty allows no legal means by which South Africa, or any other state, can be suspended or excluded without its consent.

Another threat comes from the changing nature of science itself. In recent years, science in general has been progressively transformed from a largely individualistic activity into a mainly collective enterprise. The scientist working out his ideas alone in his laboratory has been replaced by teams organized by committees. Antarctic science has always been essentially col-lective, so this change in itself should not affect it much but the increasing bureaucracy that goes with modern collective science may weaken the Antarctic spirit. Shackleton took a primitive wireless receiver, which in the event did not work, with him on the *Endurance*, but with the greatest reluctance because he felt that it gave sponsors and committees at home the means to issue directions and interfere with his handling of operations in the ice. That was perhaps an extreme attitude and it would have saved him much bother if he had had a transmitter that worked, instead of the receiver.

Even in the 1970s a scientist could feel on his own in Antarctica and the thought that he must depend on his own mental resources and the strictly limited equipment, books and papers he had brought with him was a spur to effort and innovation. Now, via satellites, there can be instantaneous direct communication between him and supervisors in the home country. This, with increasing automation of recording instruments and the necessity to comply with safety regulations and complex logistic time-tables, means that the Antarctic scientist is no longer a free agent to respond to the opportunities and nuances presented to him by the environment.

These developments in communications and support undoubtedly make for greater efficiency in collecting data and many kinds of research would be impossible without them, but they do tend to undermine the robust commonsense and self-reliance which has characterized Antarctic science in the past. Already there is a feeling among scientists that administrators are taking over the running of national Antarctic programmes. Those who are better at administration than research naturally tend to inherit the senior positions and more of the available funds tend to be devoted to projects which are politically impressive and which can be carried out by biddable technicians in the place of scientists of independent mind. Politics and bureaucracy, which those who launched the Antarctic programmes of the IGY were at such pains to keep at arm's length, could so easily infiltrate the Antarctic Treaty system and bring it down to the ineffectual and wasteful level of most international endeavour.

The great interest shown in Antarctica by conservationists has not been an unmixed blessing. Their idea that the continent should be left inviolate as a world park of wilderness is an admirable one which most Antarctic scientists would favour in principle. However, organizations such as Greenpeace have been antagonistic to the Treaty system. Initially, perhaps, this was because some stations have been undeniably careless in rubbish disposal or in the siting of installations in relation to bird and seal breeding areas. The irritation of the Antarctic establishment at such criticism is aggravated by incursions of conservationists who disrupt work by confrontational tactics but whom they would feel morally bound to succour if they got into difficulties. Consequently, conservationists have allied themselves with the non-Treaty states in agitating for United Nations jurisdiction over Antarctica. Were this to succeed it would be unlikely to be for the good of the Antarctic. The ineffectiveness of the International Whaling Commission in preserving whale stocks is an example of what can happen when a conservation organization is run by politicians who can choose to ignore scientific advice. The recent movement in Greenpeace towards establishing itself on a firmer scientific basis and the excellent books[144] on Antarctica which have been written by supporters of the conservationist cause give hope that a more pragmatic approach will prevail in the end. There will have to be compromise. Information from Antarctica is essential for the proper understanding and management of global processes, and this cannot be obtained without some airstrips and other blots on the landscape.

Two further complications in the Antarctic problem are tourism and expeditions purely for adventure. On the one hand, one would wish as many people as possible to experience the awe-inspiring beauty of this part of our world and there is no better testing ground for character and technique than the Antarctic. On the other, points of interest for tourists coincide with suitable breeding grounds for penguins and seals and they with the best sites for stations. Enormous as Antarctica is, such places are very few and the impact of inquisitive visitors both on the fragile ecosystem and the work of the scientists is correspondingly great. It seems that, already, the number of tourists in Antarctica during the summer exceeds the number of scientists and their supporting technicians. Well-planned adventures such as David Lewis's solo voyage under sail into the Antarctic ice, the Transglobe expedition, the Joint Services expeditions to Elephant and Brabant Islands, and the 'In the Footsteps of Scott' expedition have been enormously impressive extensions of human experience.[145] The danger is that the very success of these will encourage others less well prepared and equipped to chance their arm in what will always be the most dangerous seas and terrain on earth. Both tourists and adventure-seekers ultimately depend on the Antarctic professionals for help if they get into trouble. The Antarctic tradition has always been to spare no effort in going to the assistance of someone in need and in the long run this has evened out and been of advantage to all the Treaty nations. Help will not be withheld for a tourist ship or plane or an adventure expedition, but in the nature of things this imposes a responsibility and expenditure of effort, resources and possibly life which cannot be repaid, and there is resentment that it should be assumed to be available by people who take the risk in pursuit of personal pleasure, fame or profit. This problem is likely to get more acute and it is difficult to see how it can be solved.

From the ramifications of Antarctic politics we should return to the science. The value of science in the Antarctic is doubtfully in food, oil or valuable minerals, but certainly in the data which it produces. The information exported from the far south is essential for our understanding of the processes which make our world what it is and which may change it for the better or worse in the future. Surprisingly, it is perhaps the philosophy of Antarctic science that is even more important here than the facts themselves, a philosophy that regards the world as a whole, as a single system in which all the parts and processes are intermeshed with each other. The discoverers of Antarctica had their specialisms but were men of wide

A paraselena, Halley Bay (oil)

outlook, interested in all facts of the polar scene. Cook was a supreme navigator, but he helped to start the study of Pacific ethnology and experimented on the formation of ice in seawater. Bellingshausen, too, was primarily a navigator but made some of the first observations on the habits of zooplankton, and Ross, an authority on geomagnetism, was an assiduous collector of marine animal life.

One of the dominant scientific figures of the early nineteenth century, the German Alexander von Humboldt, although he never got to the Antarctic himself, was a powerful influence in the planning of the early expeditions and an advocate of the holistic approach. He believed that the world should be studied and can only be understood by systematic measurements of phenomena – magnetism, temperature, winds or currents over its entire surface. This is the opposite of the reductionist approach which holds that progress in science is only possible by concentrating on things one at a time, in isolation and under carefully controlled conditions. In the course of the nineteenth century the reductionist approach came to dominate and Humboldtian holism was almost forgotten. It persisted in Antarctic science only because the expense of a voyage to the far south made it sensible to do as much as possible and take scientists of different sorts – geologists, oceanographers, meteorologists, physicists and biologists – who all, perforce, had to make comparisons between Antarctica and the rest of the world. So, although there has not been a great deal of cross-fertilization between the sciences, they have remained aware of each other and the global view has persisted; books on Antarctic science cover the whole gamut of the sciences.

In recent years there has been a growing realization that to know more and more about less and less is a recipe for disaster when trying to deal with environmental problems. A result established in the artificial conditions of the laboratory may be misleading if one tries to apply it under natural conditions where the process one thinks one knows something about is interacting with and influenced by all sorts of other processes. Reductionism is an essential part of science and must not be decried, but it needs the discipline of holism before it can be used effectively in the real world. Together with space travel and satellite scanning, Antarctic science has played a leading role in re-establishing the view that our world must be thought of as a single entity. The symbol of Antarctica as the keystone of Gondwanaland finds expression in the present-day reality of the linkage of the south polar regions with the rest of the world through the ionosphere, atmosphere and hydrosphere, and the dominant role which they play in controlling climate and the circulation of the oceans. The Antarctic is proving to be perhaps the best place for monitoring the health of the planet, as illustrated most dramatically by the ozone 'hole' which develops over it in the spring, giving the first definite indication that pollution is having effects on the atmosphere which will have dire consequences for us all. Antarctic science has given us a warning to mend our ways before it is too late.

Antarctica is frequently described as 'a continent for science', but it has more to offer than scientific data and hypotheses. The wilderness has always been the place to which man has retired to ruminate on his place in the scheme of things, and Antarctica is the ultimate wilderness. For many who go there, the impact of the austere beauty and vast prospect of the Antarctic is profound, giving an awareness of realms beyond science. This is a recurring theme in Antarctic literature. It is epitomized in the inscription on Captain Scott's memorial, *Laesivit Arcana Poli Videt Dei* (In seeking to unveil the Pole, he found the hidden face of God) and it can be found expressed in other ways in the writings of some present-day scientists.[146]

In Chapter Two (see page 72) reference was made to the views of Pyne[53], one of the few who has attempted a humanistic study of Antarctica. He sees the ice as an emptiness that intensifies the human experience brought to it, a blank canvas which invites man to paint upon it his deepest patterns of meaning. Antarctica seems to have something infinitely precious to give to our materialistic society, but already an arrogant faith in the supremacy of technology is interposing a barrier between us and the vision it evokes. As Forbush is made to remark in Billing's novel[97]: 'It's a place for great thoughts and ideals but hardly anybody who goes there has them any more.' Perhaps the artist can help to save us from this loss. The extrovert eye of the camera gives us an idea of the beauty and wildness of the Antarctic scene, but records only what is physically there. A painting, which is an expression of the interaction of the human spirit with the natural world, may tell us more of what we should be looking for in Antarctica. We hope this book will help towards that.

Notes on Sources and Further Reading

Chapter One **Discovery**

1   General accounts of Antarctica are given by:
Antarctica: Great Stories from the Frozen Continent, Reader's Digest Services Pty Limited, Surry Hills, NSW, Australia, 1985
    H. G. R. King, *The Antarctic*, Blandford Press, London, 1969
    D. Sugden, *Arctic and Antarctic: a Modern Geographical Synthesis*, Basil Blackwell, Oxford, 1982
    D. W. H. Walton (ed.), *Antarctic Science*, Cambridge University Press, 1987
2   S. P. Smith, *Hawaiki: the original home of the Maori; with a sketch of Polynesian history*, Whitcombe & Tombs Ltd, Christchurch, New Zealand, 1910
3   The complete passage relating this episode is quoted by C. Neider, *Beyond Cape Horn: Travels in the Antarctic*, Sierra Club Books, San Francisco, 1980, pp.294–9
4   N. J. W Thrower (ed.), *The Three Voyages of Edmond Halley in the Paramore 1698–1701*, The Hakluyt Society, London, 1981
5   Reprinted as a facsimile of the 1842 edition of W. R. Chambers of Edinburgh: *The Life and Adventures of Peter Wilkins shipwrecked at the South Pole*, Review Publications Pty Ltd, Dubbo, NSW, Australia, 1979
6   J. C. Beaglehole (ed.), *The Journals of Captain James Cook*, vol. II *The Voyage of the Resolution and Adventure, 1772–1775*, Cambridge University Press for the Hakluyt Society, 1969, p.323
7   James Cook, *A Voyage towards the South Pole, and Round the World*, vol. II, London, 1777, p.293
8   Samuel Taylor Coleridge, *The Rime of the Ancient Mariner*, illustrations by Gustave Doré, Dover Publications Inc, New York, 1970
9   See note 7, p.243
10   J. R. Forster, *Observations made during a Voyage Round the World*, London, 1778, p.163
11   An officer of the sealer *George* writing in 1821. Quoted by A. G. E. Jones, 'New voyage to the South Shetlands in 1819–20', *Antarctic*, 6 (2), 1971, pp.63–6
12   J. Weddell, *A Voyage towards the South Pole Performed in the Years 1822–24* London, 1825. Reprinted by David & Charles (Publishers) Ltd, Newton Abbot, Devon, 1970
13   Captain Edmund Fanning, *Voyages & Discoveries in the South Seas 1792–1832*, Marine Research Society, Salem, Massachusetts, 1924, p.219
14   James Eights, 'On the ice-bergs of the Ant-Arctic Sea', *American Quarterly Journal of Agricultural Science*, 4 (1), 1846, pp.20–4
15   A. G. E. Jones, *Antarctica Observed: Who Discovered the Antarctic Continent?* Caedmon of Whitby, Whitby, Yorks, 1982
16   F. Debenham (ed.), *The Voyage of Captain Bellingshausen to the Antarctic Seas 1819–1821*, Hakluyt Society, 1945. Reprinted by Kraus Reprint Limited, Germany
17   P. I. Mitterling, *America in the Antarctic to 1840*, University of Illinois Press, Urbana, 1959, pp.45–51

18   A good account of the Enderbys and the voyages of their ships is given in the Reader's Digest *Antarctica* – see note 1
    For an appreciation of Biscoe see A. Savours, 'John Biscoe, Master Mariner 1794–1843', *Polar Record*, 21, pp.485–91. Biscoe's journal is reproduced in part in G. Murray, *The Antarctic Manual for the use of the expedition of 1901*, Royal Geographical Society, London, 1901
19   J. S.-C. Dumont d'Urville, *Voyage au Pole Sud et dans l'Océanie sur les corvettes l'Astrolabe et la Zelée* (10 volumes), Gide et Cie, Paris, 1847
    An abridged English translation is now available:
    H. Rosenman (trans. and ed.), *Two Voyages to the South Seas by Jules S.-C. Dumont d'Urville* (2 volumes), Melbourne University Press, 1987
20   H. J. Viola and C. Margolis (eds.), *Magnificent Voyagers: The US Exploring Expedition, 1838–1842*, Smithsonian Institution Press, Washington, DC, 1985
21   D. B. Tyler, *The Wilkes Expedition*, American Philosophical Society, Philadelphia, 1968
22   Captain Sir James Clark Ross, *A voyage of discovery and research in the southern and Antarctic regions during the years 1839–43*, John Murray, 1847. Reprinted by David & Charles, Newton Abbot, Devon, 1969, Vol. 1, p.192
23   Letter from J. E. Davis, 2nd Master of HMS *Terror*, off Cape Horn, 1 April 1842, to his sister. Archives of the Royal Botanic Gardens, Kew
24   Manuscript of a lecture by J. D. Hooker given at Swansea, 17 June 1846. Archives of the Royal Botanic Gardens, Kew
25   Narrative written by C. J. Sullivan for James Savage, Sailor on board HMS *Erebus*, Rio de Janeiro, 19 June 1843. Archives of the Royal Botanic Gardens, Kew
26   See note 22, vol. 2, pp.169–70
27   Concise accounts of these and other Antarctic expeditions from 1772 to 1955 are given in V. C. Bushnell 'History of Antarctic Exploration and Scientific Investigation' *Antarctic Map Folio Series*, no.19, American Geographical Society, New York, 1975

Chapter Two **Exploration of the Continent**

28   The personal narrative of the origins of the British National Antarctic Expedition 1901–4, *Antarctic Obsession* by Sir Clements Markham (Bluntisham Books & Erskine Press, Alburgh, Harleston, Norfolk, 1986), gives a vivid picture of some of the intrigue and argument that went on
29   F. A. Cook, *Through the First Antarctic Night*, William Heinemann, London, 1900
30   C. E. Borchgrevink, *First on the Antarctic Continent*, Georges Newnes Ltd, London, 1901. Reprinted by C. Hurst & Co, London, 1980
31   R. F. Scott, *The Voyage of the 'Discovery'*, Smith, Elder and Co, London, 1905. Reprinted by John Murray, London, 1929
32   E. von Drygalski, *Zum Kontinent des eisigen Sudens*, Georg Reimer, Berlin, 1904. English translation by M. M.

Raraty, *The Southern Ice-Continent*, Bluntisham Books & Erskine Press, Alburgh, Harleston, Norfolk, 1989.

33 O. Nordenskjöld and J. G. Andersson, *Antarctica: or Two Years Amongst the Ice of the South Pole*, Hurst and Blackett, London, 1905

34 R. N. Rudmose Brown, J. H. H. Pirie and R. C. Mossman, *The Voyage of the Scotia*, William Blackwood & Sons, Edinburgh and London, 1906. Reprinted by C. Hurst & Co, London, 1978

35 J.-B. Charcot, *The Voyage of the 'Why Not?' in the Antarctic*, Hodder & Stoughton, London, 1911

36 R. Amundsen, *The South Pole*, John Murray, London, 1912. Reprinted by C. Hurst & Co, London, 1976

37 L. Huxley (ed.), *Scott's Last Expedition* (2 volumes), Smith, Elder & Co, London, 1913

A. Cherry-Garrard, *The Worst Journey in the World*, Chatto & Windus, London, 1922; new edition 1965

38 Perhaps the best life of Scott is E. Huxley, *Scott of the Antarctic*, Weidenfeld & Nicolson, London, 1977

39 R. Huntford, *Scott and Amundsen*, Hodder & Stoughton, London, 1979

40 R. A. Priestley, *Antarctic Adventure: Scott's Northern Party*, T. Fisher Unwin, London, 1914. Reprinted by C. Hurst & Co, London, 1974

H. G. R. King (ed.), *The Wicked Mate: the Antarctic Diary of Victor Campbell*, Bluntisham Books, Erskine Press, Alburgh, Harleston, Norfolk, 1988

41 E. Shackleton, *South*, Heinemann, London, 1919

F. A. Worsley, *The Great Antarctic Rescue: Shackleton's Boat Journey*, Times Books, London, 1977

R. W. Richards, *The Ross Sea Shore Party 1914–17*, Scott Polar Research Institute, Cambridge, 1962

and a second-hand but splendid account:

A. Lansing, *Endurance: Shackleton's Incredible Voyage*, Granada Publishing Ltd, London, 1959

42 A. Hardy, *Great Waters*, Harper & Row, New York & Evanston, 1967, gives a complete list of the reports

43 H. Fletcher, *Antarctic Days with Mawson*, Angus & Robertson, London & Sydney, 1984

44 R. E. Byrd, *Little America*, G. P. Putnam's Sons, New York and London, 1930, pp.49, 342

45 L. Ellsworth, *Beyond Horizons*, The Book League of America, Inc., New York, 1938

46 Excellent accounts of Operation Highjump and other American Antarctic expeditions up to IGY are given in J. K. Bertrand *Americans in Antarctica: 1775–1948*, American Geographical Society, New York, 1971

47 Frank Debenham, *In the Antarctic*, John Murray, London, 1952, p.75

48 Ibid, p.109

49 *1910–1916 Antarctic Photographs: Herbert Ponting & Frank Hurley*, Introduction by Jennie Boddington, Macmillan, London, 1979

50 H. G. R. King, 'Heroic painter of the Antarctic', *Geographical Magazine*, 48, 1976, pp.212–17

51 Quoted on the dust-cover of the 1965 edition of *The Worst Journey in the World* – see note 37

52 Eliot Porter, *Antarctica*, Hutchinson, London, 1978

Eric Hosking, *Antarctic Wildlife*, Croom Helm, London and Canberra, 1982

53 Stephen Pyne, *The Ice: a Journey to Antarctica*, University of Iowa Press, 1986

54 See note 42

55 J. Coleman-Cooke, *Discovery II in the Antarctic*, Odhams Press Ltd, London, 1963, p.208

56 Quoted in 'Recognise it?' *Antarctic*, 4 (4), 1965, p.213

57 Maurice Conly, *Ice on my Palette*, Whitcoulls Publishers, Christchurch, New Zealand, 1977

58 David Smith, 'The artistic challenge of Antarctica', *Geographical Magazine*, 53, 1981, pp.884–9

Chapter Three Gateways to Antarctica

59 J. M. Ross, *Ross in the Antarctic*, Caedmon of Whitby, Whitby, Yorkshire, 1982

60 The useful term 'peri-Antarctic' has been introduced by R. K. Headland in *Chronological list of Antarctic expeditions and related historical events*, Cambridge University Press 1989.

Australian Antarctic expeditions have been described by P. Law in *Antarctic Odyssey*, Heinemann, Melbourne, Auckland and London, 1983

61 E. Wilson, *Diary of the Terra Nova Expedition to the Antarctic 1910–1912*, edited by H. G. R. King, Blandford Press, London, 1972, p.60

62 Ibid, p.62

63 A vivid description of the flight from Christchurch to Williams Field is given by M. Parfit in *South Light: a Journey to Antarctica*, Bloomsbury Publishing Ltd, London, 1988

64 Information on Antarctic tourism is given in the Reader's Digest *Antarctica* (see note 1) and by P. D. Hart, 'The growth of Antarctic tourism', *Oceanus*, 31, 1988, pp.93–100

65 C. Swithinbank, 'Antarctic Airways: Antarctica's first commercial airline', *Polar Record*, 24, 1988, pp.313–16

66 R. D. Keynes (ed.), *The Beagle Record*, Cambridge University Press, 1979, p.190

67 Ibid, p.191

68 Ian J. Strange, *The Falkland Islands and their Natural History*, David & Charles, Newton Abbot, Devon, 1987

Illustrations and descriptions of the birds of the Southern Atlantic are also given in HRH The Duke of Edinburgh, *Birds from Britannia*, Longman Group Ltd, London, 1962

69 T. W. Smith *A Narrative of the Life, Travels and Sufferings of Thomas W. Smith ... Written by Himself*, W. C. Hill, Boston, 1844 (see page 91 for full title)

70 For an assessment of the economic potentialities see E. A. A. Shackleton, 'Falkland Islands economic study', *Command Paper* 8653, HMSO, London, 1982

71 A. R. Michaelis, 'The Falkland Islands: the ideal Antarctic base', *Interdisciplinary Science Reviews*, 13, 1988, pp.1–4

Chapter Four The Southern Ocean

72 G. Deacon, *The Antarctic Circumpolar Ocean*, Cambridge University Press, 1984

73 For further information on the marine biology of the Southern Ocean see Walton, note 1; R. M. Laws, (ed.) *Antarctic Ecology* (2 volumes), Academic Press, London, 1984; and W. N. Bonner and D. W. H. Walton (eds.), *Key Environments: Antarctica*, Pergamon Press, Oxford, 1985

74 For summaries on the biology of whales see R. Gambell, *Key Environments: Antarctica*, Pergamon Press, Oxford, 1985, pp.223–41; and S. G. Brown and C. H. Lockyer, 'Whales', *Antarctic Ecology*, vol. 2, Academic Press, London, 1984.

The work on buoyancy control in the sperm whale is described by M. R. Clarke in *Journal of the Marine Biological Association of the United Kingdom*, 58, 1978, pp.27–71
75 See note 12
76 Edward Wilson, *Diary of the Discovery Expedition*, Blandford Press, London, 1966, p.74
77 M. Minnaert, *The Nature of Light and Colour in the Open Air*, Dover Publications Inc., 1954. This gives the physical background of the colour effects mentioned here as well as of mirages, parhelia and other phenomena seen in the Antarctic
78 See note 61, p.74
79 See note 53 for more information about ice and icebergs

Chapter Five The Island of South Georgia

80 See note 7, p.213
81 See note 69, p.136
82 Robert Cushman Murphy, *Logbook for Grace*, Robert Hale Ltd, London, 1947, pp.141, 142, 143–4
83 The history of the British Antarctic Survey is to be found in V. Fuchs, *Of Ice and Men*, Anthony Nelson, Oswestry, Shropshire, 1982
84 See Walton, note 1
85 Nan Brown, *Antarctic Housewife*, Hutchinson, London, 1971
86 E. Mickleburgh, *Beyond the Frozen Sea: Visions of Antarctica*, The Bodley Head, London, 1987

An excellent general account of Bird Island is given by D. F. Parmelee in *Bird Island in Antarctic Waters*, University of Minnesota Press, Minneapolis, 1980
87 J. P. Croxall and P. A. Prince, 'Food, feeding ecology and ecological segregation of seabirds at South Georgia', *Biological Journal of the Linnean Society*, 14, 1980, pp.103–31.
88 R. Headland, *The Island of South Georgia*, Cambridge University Press, 1984

R. Perkins, *Operation Paraquat: the Battle for South Georgia*, Picton Publishing (Chippenham) Ltd, Beckington, near Bath, Somerset, 1986
89 See note 70

Chapter Six The Antarctic Archipelagos

90 Ian Cameron, *The White Ship*, Pan Books, London, 1978
91 For general accounts of the South Sandwich Islands see S. Kemp and A. L. Nelson, 'The South Sandwich Islands', *Discovery Reports*, vol. III, 1931, pp.133–98

M. W. Holdgate and P. E. Baker, 'The South Sandwich Islands. I. General description', *British Antarctic Survey, Scientific Reports*, no.91, 1979 (76 pp.)

For the Argentine episode see Perkins, note 88
92 See Walton, note 1
93 See note 6, p.638
94 J. W. S. Marr, 'The South Orkney Islands', *Discovery Reports*, vol. X, 1935, pp.283–382

D. Rootes (ed.), *A concise account of Signy Island Base H.*, British Antarctic Survey, Cambridge, 1988

95 Quoted in J. Sparks and T. Soper, *Penguins*, David & Charles, Newton Abbot, Devon, 1967. This book should also be consulted for general information about penguins
96 B. Stonehouse, *Animals of the Antarctic: the Ecology of the Far South*, Peter Lowe, 1972, is a good general introduction to the sea mammals and birds of the Antarctic
97 G. Billing, *Forbush and the Penguins*, A. H. & A. W. Reed, Wellington, Auckland, Sydney, 1965
98 E. Shackleton, *South*, William Heinemann, London, 1922. Abridged edition, p.70
99 F. D. Ommanney, *South Latitude*, Longman, Green & Co, London, 1938
100 C. Furse, *Elephant Island: an Antarctic Expedition*, Anthony Nelson, Shrewsbury, 1979
101 W. H. B. Webster, *Narrative of a Voyage to the Southern Atlantic Ocean in the Years 1828, 29, 30, performed in H.M. Sloop Chanticleer*, (2 volumes), 1834. Reprinted by Dawsons of Pall Mall, London, 1970

Chapter Seven The Antarctic Peninsula

102 See Walton, note 1
103 C. Furse, *Antarctic Year: Brabant Island Expedition*, Croom Helm, London, 1986
104 For descriptions of life at Palmer Station and aboard the *Hero* see notes 3 and 63
105 See note 35, p.209
106 See note 3, p.325
107 J. Rymill, *Southern Lights: the Official Account of the British Graham Land Expedition 1934–1937*, The Travel Book Club, London, 1939

C. Bertram, *Antarctica, Cambridge, Conservation and Population*, privately printed, 1987
108 'Recent discoveries in the Antarctic Ocean. From the Log-book of the Brig Tula, commanded by Mr John Biscoe, RN Communicated by Messrs Enderby', *Journal of the Royal Geographical Society*, 3, 1833, pp.105–12
109 Jennie Darlington, *My Antarctic Honeymoon*, Frederick Muller Ltd, London, 1957, pp.131–2
110 Two books devoted to the achievements of women in Antarctica are:

E. Chipman, *Women on the Ice; A History of Women in the Far South*, Melbourne University Press, 1986

B. Land, *The New Explorers: Women in Antarctica*, Dodd, Mead & Co, New York, 1981

A graphic and entertaining account by one of the first women to work in Antarctica is given by Pamela Young, *Penguin Summer – or a Rare Bird in Antarctica*, A. H. & A. W. Reed, Wellington, New Zealand, 1971
111 See note 109, p.139
112 N. W. M. Orr, 'Physiology of sledge dogs', *Antarctic Research*, (ed. R. Priestley, R. J. Adie and G. de Q. Robin,) Butterworths, London, 1965, pp.61–70. Most books on Antarctic explorations devote a fair amount of attention to dogs but R. Dovers, *Huskies*, G. Bell & Sons, London, 1957, does so in particular

Chapter Eight The Ice Shelves

113 See note 83, p.231
114 R. E. Byrd, *Alone*, G. P. Putnam's Sons, New York, 1938, p.83

115 See Walton, note 1

116 Among the more readable accounts of the ozone hole are Walton, note 1; J. Gribbin, 'The hole in the sky', *Scope*, 12, Summer 1988, pp.4–8; R.S. Stolarski, 'The Antarctic ozone hole', *Scientific American*, 258 (1), 1988, pp.20–6

An account by the man who started the present alarm is in J. C. Farman, 'Recent measurements of total ozone at British Antarctic Survey stations', *Philosophical Transactions of the Royal Society of London*, Series A, 323, 1987, pp.629–44

117 See notes 95 and 96

Beautiful drawings of emperor penguins are to be found in E. Wilson, *Birds of the Antarctic*, (ed. B. Roberts), Blandford Press, London, 1967

Chapter Nine The Continent of Antarctica

118 V. Fuchs and E. Hillary, *The Crossing of Antarctica*, Cassell, London, 1958

119 R. Fiennes, *To the Ends of the Earth*, Hodder & Stoughton, London, 1983

120 P. Siple, *90° South: the Story of the American South Pole Conquest*, G. P. Putnam's Sons, New York, 1959

121 An account of Soviet IGY work is given by W. Sullivan, in *Assault on the Unknown*, McGraw-Hill Book Company Inc., New York, 1961

122 See Walton, note 1; R. Fifield, *International Research in the Antarctic*, Oxford University Press, 1987

123 See Walton, note 1; note 53; Fifield, note 122

124 See note 31, p.627

125 See Porter, note 52

A description of the aesthetics of dry valleys is given by Pyne, note 53

Physiographic descriptions and information about weathering, soils and microbiology are to be found in I.B. Campbell and G. G. C. Claridge, *Antarctica: Soils, Weathering Processes and Environment*, Elsevier, Amsterdam, 1987

126 R. B. Heywood, 'Inland Waters' *Antarctic Ecology*, (ed. R. M. Laws), vol. 1, Academic Press, London, 1984, pp.279–344

W. F. Vincent, 'Antarctic limnology', *Inland Waters of New Zealand*, (ed. A. B. Viner), Science Information Publishing Centre, New Zealand, 1987

127 R. W. Johnson and P. M. Smith, 'Antarctic research and lunar exploration', *Advances in Space Science and Technology*, 10, Academic Press, New York, 1970, pp.1–44

Chapter Ten Hope out of Antarctica?

128 F. O. Vicuna (ed.), *Antarctic Resources Policy. Scientific, Legal and Political Issues*, Cambridge University Press, 1983

A. Parsons, *Antarctica: the Next Decade*, Report of a study group (Chairman Sir Anthony Parsons), Cambridge University Press, 1987

129 W. J. Morgan, D. B. Tyler, J. L. Leonhart and M. F. Loughlin (eds.), *Autobiography of Rear Admiral Charles Wilkes, US Navy 1798–1877*, Naval History Division, Department of the Navy, Washington, 1978, p.376

130 See Huntford, note 39, pp.479–508

131 *The Diaries of Captain Robert Scott*, vol VI, Sledging Diaries November 1911–March 1912. Facsimile, University Microfilms Ltd, 1968

132 G. Hattersley-Smith (ed.), *The Norwegian with Scott: Tryggve Gran's Antarctic Diary 1910–1913*, National Maritime Museum, HMSO, 1984

133 See Huntford, note 39, pp.561–79

134 E. W. Hunter Christie, *The Antarctic Problem: An Historical and Political Study*, George Allen & Unwin Ltd, London, 1951

P. J. Beck, *The International Politics of Antarctica*, Croom Helm, London and Sydney, 1986

135 See Beck, note 134

136 See Sullivan, note 121

137 See Beck, note 134

138 See, for example, King and Walton, note 1; Mickleburgh, note 86; Parsons, note 128

The record is *Antarctica: a Portrait in Wildlife and Natural Sound*, Saydisc Specialized Recordings Ltd, 1971

139 See Beck, note 134

G. D. Triggs (ed.), *The Antarctic Treaty Regime: Law, Environment and Resources*, Cambridge University Press, 1987

Antarctic Treaty System: an Assessment; Proceedings of a Workshop held at Beardmore South Field Camp, Antarctica, January 7–13, 1985, National Academy Press, Washington DC, 1986

140 An account of the work of SCAR is given by Fifield, note 122

141 The text of this convention is given by Mickleburgh note 86, and it is discussed in Vicuna, note 128, Parsons, note 128, and Triggs, note 139

142 Mineral exploitation is discussed in Vicuna, note 128, Parsons, note 128, and Triggs, note 139. The Convention (CRAMRA) is described and discussed by P. J. Beck, 'Convention on the Regulation of Antarctic Mineral Resource Activities: a major addition to the Antarctic Treaty System', *Polar Record*, 25, 1989, pp.19–32

143 See Beck, note 134

P. J. Beck, 'Antarctica's smile annual ritual? The United Nations and Antarctica 1987', *Polar Record*, 24, 1988, pp.207–12

144 See Mickleburgh, note 86

B. Brewster, *Antarctica: Wilderness at Risk*, A. H. & A. W. Reed Ltd, Wellington, New Zealand (for Friends of the Earth), 1982

J. May, *The Greenpeace Book of Antarctica: a New View of the Seventh Continent*, Dorling Kindersley, London, 1988

145 D. Lewis, *Ice Bird: the First Single-Handed Voyage to Antarctica*, Collins, London, 1975

Fiennes, note 119

Furse, notes 100 and 103

R. Mear and R. Swan *In the Footsteps of Scott*, Jonathan Cape, London, 1987

146 For example, see A. Hayter, *The Year of the Quiet Sun: One Year at Scott Base, Antarctica: a Personal Impression*, Hodder & Stoughton, London, 1968, p.187; Law, note 60, p.239

J. Reynolds, *Going South: an Antarctic Experience*, Marshall Pickering, Basingstoke, Hants, 1986, is in a rather different category, since the author's convictions were preconceived rather than evoked by Antarctica

Index